VIETNAM : 1982 – 2017

RUINS TO INCREDIBLE PROGRESS

VIETNAM : 1982 – 2017
RUINS TO INCREDIBLE PROGRESS

Geetesh Sharma

Edited by:
Prem Kapoor
Kusum Jain

BANYAN TREE BOOKS PVT. LTD.

ISBN : 978-81-937285-0-5

Price : 899

First edition : 2018

Published by :
Banyan Tree Books Pvt. Ltd.
7/31, Ansari Road, Daryaganj
New Delhi-110 002 (India)
www.rajkamalprakashan.com

Printed at :
B.K. Offset
Naveen Shahdara, Delhi-110 032

President of the National Assembly of the Socialist Republic of Vietnam NGUYEN THI KIM NGAN.

Dedicated to :

H. E. Ms. Nguyen Thi Kim Ngan
Hon'ble Chairperson, National Assembly of S. R. Vietnam
who had been an inspiring and motivating force
behind this book.

FEW WORDS...

I have been acquainted with the reputation of the Indian journalist Geetesh Sharma through his various publications, espeially as a friend of Vietnam and the Chairman of the Indo - Vietnam Solidarity Committee. I could feel the profound love he has retained towards Vietnam, may be just ranked 2nd after his homeland India. Therefore, I am deeply impressed by the draft of his book named "Vietnam : 1982 - 2017, Ruins to Incredible Progress."

The book honestly reflects the length of time and the width of space during his 28 visits to Vietnam from 1982 to 2017. He has meticulously explored from small villages in the northwest mountainous areas to the busting Ho Chi Minh City, a bustling city as well as other 40 provinces of Vietnam. He has observed a remarkable transformation of Da Nang from a "fishermen's village" in 1982 to "an incredible city" in 2017 (Chapter 5). He also discovered that in 1982, bicycles and cyclos were the means of transportation, which, as of 2016 were kept as just memory souvenirs.

Though, he also ponders over the diffculties that Vietnam has encountered and what needs to be done to improve the relation between Vietnam and India. In his book, we can see the paradoxes lying in our relation. The first is despite our long-lasting and close-knit relation for millennia, why has the name "Vietnam" been fading in the minds of the Indians during the era of rapid and accessible communication? The second is, in the ancient time, the bilateral Vietnam - India trade was flourishing despite limited resources, why is it so far behind now? And the same happen with tourism, cultural exchange, literatur, philosophy, politics and people-to-people exchange. In my opinion, the writer of this book is not only a passionate Vietnam-lover but also a man with fierce thoughts and actions.

We highly appreciate his passion for knowledge and his heartfelt comments. We might not agree with him at some points but there is one thing we should be difinitely that we should together crack the paradoxes to bring the once-glorious relationship for millennia into a new era, in accordance with the spiritual and noble sentiment between our two countries.

To achieve the above goal, we would further strengthen and promote cultural cooperation between our two countries. Consequently, this book could be a boat carrying cultural messengers, contributing to the promotion of the close-knit cooperation between our countries and peoples. In that spirit, the book written by the journalist Geetesh Sharma will be a highly desirable publication.

Hanoi 23nd November, 2017

Dr. Truong Minh Tuan
Minister of Information and Communications
The Socialist Republic of Vietnam
Chairman of the Vietnam - India Friendship Association

ACKNOWLEDGEMENTS

- I am indebted to H. E. Mr. Truong Minh Tuan, Hon'ble Minister of Information & Communications, and Chairman, Vietnam Union of Friendship Organisations, S. R. Vietnam for his valued support.
- I offer my sincere thanks to Mr. Ajay Panot, Mr. Ashok Sharda, Mr. Dilbagh Man Mohan Singh, Mr. G. N. Tiwary, Mr. M. B. Radhakrishnan and of course Indian Business Chamber (INCHAM) in Vietnam, Ho Chi Minh City for their indispensable help and co-operation.
- Ms. Pravamayee Samantaray, Lecturer in English, Kendrapara Autonomous College, Kendrapara and Mr. Ashok Verma deserve my special thanks for their spirited assistance.
- My thanks are also due to Mr. Nguyen Dang Chinh, Vietnam News Agency, Mr. Nguyen Trong , DDG, Central Commission for External Relations, CPV, Tran Duc Minh, VUFO, Ms. Nguyen T.K. VAN, working in the office of Party Commission for External affairs for their valued co-operation.
- My gratitude is also due to Mr. Ashok Maheshwari, the publisher.
- Last but not the least my thanks are due to Mr. Prem Kapoor and Ms. Kusum Jain for their most valued assistance in editing this book.

CONTENTS

VIETNAM : 1982 – 2017
RUINS TO INCREDIBLE PROGRESS

1

WHY VIETNAM?

My emotional attachment with Vietnam had started in February 1958 when President Ho Chi Minh had visited Kolkata on the last leg of his state visit to India. I was one among the huge crowd that had gathered to felicitate and listen to him speak with rapt attention and pin drop silence. His speech in Vietnamese was translated into English and the audience, myself included, was literally charmed by his openheartedness and overwhelmed by his exemplary simplicity and austere life-style. I still cherish that memory and share it with my friends.

This incident did not only draw me towards Ho Chi minh but inspired me to know about his impressions and opinion about India in detail. When I went through his speech that he had delivered in New Delhi on 6th February 1958 wherein he mentioned and expressed his feelings about India and its people, I came to know that he was not only well versed about India and Indian conditions but he was equally concerned about India. I got several evidences of his attachment towards India and the prime evidence was his above mentioned speech a portion of which I refer hereunder :

"I suffered at seeing my brothers in Vietnam suffered and ill-treated by foreigners. I left my country (in1911). The first country I came to was India. I also found that my brothers in India (also) suffered from a foreign yoke." – President Ho Chi Minh's speech at the reception given by the president Ho Chi minh reception committee in New Delhi on February 06,1958.

In 1927 Ho Chi Minh had the occasion to meet Motilal Nehru at Brussels and they both greeted each other so warmly as if they were quite old buddies. They had a long discussion about Indo-Vietnam relations besides various other international issues. During his state visit to India in 1958 when President Ho referred this incident to Indian Prime Minister Jawahar Lal Nehru, he was astounded and conceded that his father Motilal Nehru had told him about the said meeting but he did not remember it in such a detail as President Ho had described.

I also collected another important fact about President Ho Chi Minh's visit to India in 1946 when on his way to Paris he had stopped over Calcutta for an overnight stay at Great Eastern Hotel (presently Lalit Great Eastern Hotel). Keeping aside all the protocols the President had visited the Communist Party of India's office on foot at Dacres Lane. Everybody present there was taken aback when they learnt about unalarmed arrival of President Ho Chi Minh. Mansur Habibullah had informed me about the incident in detail as he was one of the eyewitnesses. Although this incident was referred by Bhawani Sen in one of his memoirs but he mentioned a wrong date.

Needless to say that all this had a deep influence over me and which had prompted me to determine that someday I would write about my most revered personality and the great friend of India, President Ho Chi Minh and I would collect material informations in detail and would acquaint my fellow countrymen about him.

From 1971 to 1975, as a member of Indo-Vietnam Solidarity Committee, I participated in numerous processions, demonstrations and public meetings to express solidarity with the people of Vietnam and their freedom struggle. People of India, especially those of West Bengal, were so emotionally involved with Vietnam's freedom struggle that Vietnam became a household name, that reflected in the most popular slogan during those days – "your name Vietnam, my name Vietnam, our name Vietnam".

Indira Gandhi, the then Prime Minister of India, who was sincerely carrying forward the legacy of her illustrious father Jawaharlal Nehru used to address Pham Van Dong, the then Honourable Prime Minister of Vietnam as 'Uncle', that reflected how intimate they had been to each other.

In 1990 on behalf of our Indo-Vietnam Solidarity Committee, we had an opportunity to welcome, felicitate and interact with the legendary war strategist of Vietnam General Vo Nguyen Giap and his wife, when they had visited Kolkata to unveil the bust of Ho Chi Minh at the crossing of Jawaharlal Nehru Road and Ho Chi Minh Sarani.

In 1982, under the leadership of Prof. Santimoy Ray, eminent Historian and the then Secretary General of Indo-Vietnam Solidarity Committee, I had an occasion to visit Vietnam for the first time in a delegation and we extensively toured Vietnam from Hanoi to Ho Chi Minh City by road through various provinces. Since then till date I have visited Vietnam for about 28 times and have closely witnessed its journey towards development.

In 1982 I had the honour of meeting the then Prime Minister Pham Van Dong and in the subsequent period I have had the honour of being granted an audience by the General Secretaries of the Communist Party of Vietnam, State Presidents, Prime Ministers, Chairmen of People's Committees besides meeting and interacting with the common people of Vietnam. I have, in the meanwhile, written about seven books in English and Hindi (the National Language of India) on and about my experiences in Vietnam and of which three titles have since been translated and published in the Vietnamese language.

I am deeply indebted to Vietnam and am literally overwhelmed to have received love and regards in abundance besides due recognition for my contribution towards promotion of goodwill, fraternal ties and bilateral relations. In fact, it has energized me further to make still more contributions in this direction. Since last one year or so I have been constantly thinking that it is for sure that I may not be able to repay the debt of Vietnam but I should still do something for my own satisfaction.

During my meeting and interaction with H.E. Ms. Nguyen Thi Kim Ngan, the Chairperson of the National Assembly of S. R. Vietnam, I spontaneously committed myself to write a memoir at the fag end of my life, on the basis of my experiences in Vietnam from 1982 till 2017, where I may highlight how a country, nearly reduced to ruins emerged and transformed itself into a fast developing nation having provided material as well as spiritual facilities to its people ensuring a life of dignity to them, which most of the countries in Asia are deprived of. Naturally, this in itself is no less than a charisma.

Hon'ble Chairperson H.E. Ms. Ngan interrupted me and said that before writing whatever I wished to, I should visit one more time to Vietnam in 2017 along with my colleague and see for myself the contemporary Vietnam. She invited us as her guests and this very accommodative gesture thrilled me.

On her invitation we visited Vietnam and I am presenting here an account of whatever we observed as an eye witness. No, this is neither an academic nor a research work; on the contrary it is an eyewitness account and exposition of reality.

The sweet memories of Vietnam, that India once had, are unfortunately fading. This is a small but significant endeavour to recollect the past and acquaint the readers with the present day Vietnam. I believe, this venture of mine would not only bring the two peoples of India and Vietnam closer to each other but would lead to peace, progress and fraternity in the Asian region as a whole.

The then Indian Prime Minister Jawaharlal Nehru and President of Vietnam Ho Chi Minh had laid the solid foundation in modern times and had added newer dimensions to the age old traditional friendly relations between India and Vietnam during the modern times, and these relations were no more limited in the confines of economic interests and extended deep down the hearts to emotional level. When President Ho Chi Minh on his state visit to India in February 1958 landed at the Palam Airport Jawaharlal Nehru set aside all the protocols and not only hugged the visiting President but also fondled his beard. They both preferred their intimacy rather than the official protocol.

Indo-Vietnam relations have always been above party politics in India and all the political parties, irrespective of their ideologies, have always extended their wholehearted support to it.

It may not be out of place to mention here an incident of 1979. The then External Affairs Minister of India Atal Behari Vajpayee was on an official visit to China when China invaded Vietnam to teach it a lesson. The act did upset the External Affairs Minister so much that in protest he truncated his tour and came back to India.

Of late (on 3rd September 2016) when Prime Minister of India Narendra Modi was on a state visit to Vietnam, the common impression everywhere was that he was visiting a most intimate friendly nation and in a day's state visit 12 MOUs were signed between the two countries which manifested their strong friendly ties and their common urge to further strengthen the existing bonds in the coming days.

I may like to draw the attention towards a common fact, which is although known to one and all that on all the international forums, be it the U.N.O. or other regional forums both India and Vietnam have wholeheartedly supported each others' policies.

Whenever we talk of fraternity and brotherhood I am reminded of the days during 1945 to 1975, when Vietnam was engaged in its liberation struggle and the people of India in general and those of West Bengal and Kolkata (then Calcutta) in particular especially the students, youths, poets, writers, theatre personalities and intellectuals had extended moral and material support to their Vietnamese brethren. The then Congress leader Sarat Bose and the soldiers of Indian National Army had even offered to fight alongside Vietnamese freedom fighters in their struggle. This offer was although appreciated by the Vietnamese leadership but they had politely declined it.

During those days people in India and particularly in Kolkata had spontaneously demonstrated on numerous occasions in support of the liberation war of Vietnam. It was during one such demonstration that an obscure poet raised a slogan in Bengali - 'Tomar Nam, Amar Nam' (your name, my name) and thousands of throats responded in unison 'Vietnam, Vietnam'. Subsequently it became a phenomenal slogan. In fact Ho Chi Minh and Vietnam were household names in India and were most popular even in the remote villages of India besides the cities during those days.

It is, however, an irony that today when the means of communication are far more developed and easily available, the name of Vietnam is slowly fading from the hearts and minds of the people of India. What to talk of the common man even some of the enlightened people also believe that Vietnam being a communist country must be a most backward country and may not have anything to offer to the tourists.

Since 1990 Vietnam achieved an all round progress, especially in the basic infrastructure and the social structure. I believe, India should learn from the experiences of Vietnam and should apply the same according to the conditions prevailing in India.

During my various journeys to Vietnam I found that from higher authorities to common man, all had a soft corner for India and were aware about it to certain extent. However, in India the picture is different. People in India, in general, are almost ignorant about the present day Vietnam. Government to government relations although are par excellent but people to people relations are lagging far behind.

2

MY FIRST ENCOUNTER : HANOI TO HO CHI MINH CITY BY ROAD IN 1982

I may not have seen that Vietnam, whose dauntless and courageous freedom fighters had not only braved the torrent of U.S. bombing but had also tormented America at the risk of their

Ravages of war

own lives. However, during my first visit to Vietnam in 1982, I had witnessed the huge destruction and devastation caused by the U.S. through its chemical warfare, carpet bombings and Napalm bombs that destroyed thousands of hectares of agricultural land and reduced it to barrenness. When we talk about the extensive destruction and devastation that Vietnam had suffered during the war of liberation, it is very difficult to assess correctly as Vietnam

Ravages of war

had been in a continual state of war between 1939 and 1975 and during this long period of about 35 years it was invaded by the French – Japanese troops to Chang Kai-Shek troops, US troops, Australian troops, New-Zealand troops, South Korean troops and Philippine troops and that during all those invasions all kinds of weapons, excepting the nuclear ones, were used. No area was spared and even out of the way hamlets were targeted.

Some villages around Da Nang had witnessed the landing of US marines in March 1965. From 1954 to 1965 those villages had to face a series of massacres and repeated mopping up operations conducted by the Diem troops and police. Subsequently, they became the victims of concerted attacks by the US-puppet troops besides systematic bombardment by the US Air Force and the Phoenix operations from 1965 to 1975. It is nearly impossible to gauge and assess the number of victims and the extent of damage and destruction inflicted on the people, crops, schools etc.

Take for instance a town Vinh that was destroyed during the first war of resistance, was subsequently levelled by American bombing between 1965 and 1968 and was again reduced to rubble in 1972 after its reconstruction. How will one be able to sum up the devastation caused by those successive attacks?

The US administration had officially admitted that the Indo-china war had costed them 150 billion US dollars but according to other American sources the cost amounted to at least 300 billion US dollars. So, the figures in circulation and the assessment of damage and destruction is extremely confusing. One can simply say that with vast technical and financial power that they controlled, the Americans went out of their way to attain their goal. The US intelligence service was fully mobilized besides US army research centres, the services of many university laboratories were requisitioned to find out the best way of killing, destroying and corrupting.

One may easily understand the extent of US involvement in the Vietnam war with this simple fact that at the height of the war, 75 per cent of all the US land forces, 60 per cent of the US air force

A Hanoi Street in 1982

and 40 per cent of the US naval force were involved in Indochina besides of course the special forces like the 'Green Berats' trained for counter-guerrilla activities.

In 1969 the US expeditionary force comprised:

11 infantry division;
73,000 air personnel;
87,000 naval personnel;

The total number of effective deployment was around 54,300 men. It was reinforced by :

42,000 South Korean troops;
8,000 Austrailian troops;
2,000 Philippinos;
300 new Zealanders;
11,000 Thai troops;

The puppet army had a total effective strength of 1,200,000 men and the puppet police 200,000 men.

Further, the weapons that were used to destroy Vietnam were more powerful and sophisticated than those used in previous wars. For the first time in the human history chemical warfare had been conducted on such a large scale. 71,23,000 litres of Chemical compounds of the three agents, Orange (2.4-D and 2.45-T), White (2.4-D and Picloram) and Blue (cacodylic acid) had been used. This exhaustive use of chemicals caused the leaves to fall followed by the death of trees and plants. The land was denuded of trees and turned barren and took about a decade to regenerate the soil.

The massive spraying of chemicals had also destroyed birds, insects, fish, fauna and flora on vast expanses of the land.

So far as the material losses are concerned, according to an estimate :

9,000 of 15,000 hamlets were destroyed and a large number were completely destroyed.

10 million hectares of rice-fields and crops were destroyed or burnt.

Ten per cent of the land was contaminated by toxic chemicals and rendered sterile.

The war left a deep scar over Vietnamese Society as a whole. About 800,000 children were orphaned, about one million women were widowed. Nearly half a million people were left invalid and physically handicapped.

No country in the world has ever suffered so much and that too for such a long period of time.

Today Vietnam has overcome the nightmare and is steadily progressing following the ideals and guidelines of President Ho Chi Minh.

I had also witnessed the indomitable spirit of the people of Vietnam, who were brimming with determination to overcome. Although it was a trying time but the people were facing it with strong will, commitment and determination – "We shall overcome".

A Hanoi Street in 1982.

A Us Air-force bomber captured during War on display at Remnants of War Museum, Ho Chi Minh City.

Even in 1982, after 13 years of the sad demise of the great motivating leader Ho Chi Minh, I could still feel his presence among the minds and hearts of his people. I am yet to see or know about any other leader who not only kept on inspiring, encouraging and motivating his compatriots during his life time to continue their ceaseless struggle against the most powerful enemy but whose ideals and thoughts continued to inspire his people even after his death to accomplish his dream of unification of Vietnam and its national reconstruction after the unification of north and south Vietnam.

I salute President Ho Chi Minh for the indomitable spirit that he could generate among the people of Vietnam.

3

HO CHI MINH CITY TO HANOI BY ROAD AND RAILWAYS IN 2008

During my various visits, I travelled numerous places, cities, towns and villages of Vietnam. All this may not be described in a book like this, but I would like to refer in brief about the places that I visited, but avoided mention in detail in this book.

As mentioned earlier, wherever I went, I made it a point to spend more and more time to talk to the common men, sometimes I visited the houses as an unwanted guest pretending that I wanted to relieve myself. I was astonished and pleased to observe that they not only allowed me entry, but invited me at a tea or coffee and even dinner if they were having it. My intention was to see the maximum in minimum time and I may claim to have succeeded to certain extent in my mission.

In 1982 I had travelled to Ho Chi Minh City from Hanoi by road and had witnessed the devastation everywhere, caused by the French and American aggressors. I had wondered how this country would be able to overcome and stand on its feet. During my subsequent visits when I witnessed the determination of the people and the massive reconstruction work that was going on in Vietnam, I got my answer.

In 2008 when I took an assignment to write a book titled "Traces of Indian Culture in Vietnam", I decided that I must travel to those places where the foot prints of Indian culture still persist in the shape of Cham Towers, I mean the centuries' old Hindu temples. So, we (myself and Kusum Jain) decided to start our journey from Ho Chi Minh City to Da Nang by road and from there by a train to Hanoi. Trains in Vietnam are run on metre gauge rails that were laid with the help of India. In the initial stage India had also supplied rakes, wagons and locomotives to Vietnam. The train journey in Vietnam is most comfortable, safe and enjoying. All through the train journey, we were charmed by the scenic beauty of Vietnam. Through our journey we decided to visit the various sites of Cham Towers, many of which were intact while many others were in ruins, but the restoration work was in progress everywhere.

We met archaeologists from Japan, Poland, France etc., but no Indian archaeologist was there. Wherever we saw the remains of the Cham Towers, we requested our driver to stop, so that we may see.

After Ho Chi Minh City, our first halt was at Phan Tiet, a beautiful small town. At the outskirt of the town there was a Cham tower on a hill, well preserved. It seemed that somebody was worshipping there every day, may be the caretaker because we found the offerings of fresh fruits and the incense sticks were lighted. There were three temples in the complex.

We met a family in the nearby village of Phan Tiet, who claimed that their ancestors were the king of that area. They had displayed old dresses, arms and ammunitions, the crown of the king etc. in a mini private museum. They were proud of their past glory, but presently the whole family was working in an agricultural field, a small plot which they owned with no remorse. They told us with contentment that the people must cope with the situation happily. They offered us tea, coffee and snacks. Before our departure a lady whispered in my ear 'we spend a lot of money to maintain this museum. If you like, you may donate something'. Happily we contributed 20USD.

Next of our destination was Nha Trang, where there was a magnificent resort with all the modern facilities. In the background there was a mountain, in the middle Kai River was flowing and at a distance there was a sea beach. This was once the capital of one of the Hindu Kingdoms, Kauthara. There is an area called Po Nagar. A few more temples are situated here along with the main temple, the Temple of Bhagawati of Shakt Cult.

After the decline of Hindu Kingdom, the Vietnamese adopted it as their own goddess, Inu and many mythological stories were created around their Inu. According to one of such stories, Inu had initiated rice cultivation in Vietnam. Even a section of Cham Muslims worship this goddess, although there is no concept of any goddess in Islam. So, every community worships this goddess as per their Lunar Calendar, without any disharmony. They live with co-existence and tolerance.

While travelling from Phan Tiet to Nha Trang by road, one comes across a number of ruins of ancient Hindu temples or Cham Towers at about dozens of places. These temples are situated in various places from sea shore, plains, and dense forest to hill top. Our driver was very co-operative. Wherever we requested him to see the temple, he readily agreed although it lingered our journey. On our way we witnessed a Linga shaped temple erected on Yoni. This village was once called Indrapura, the capital of Bhadraverman II and was quite developed and prosperous. According to rock inscriptions, Bhadraverman II was the descendant of Sage Vrigu. Deserted by its devotees, the temple today stands isolated in the middle of a paddy field as a lone witness to its glorious past. We passed through Chien Dan Towers on our way to Da Nang which is 60 kilometres south of Da Nang. Chien Dan tower was discovered in 1989 and the Govt. of Vietnam has well-preserved this tower. It consists of three towers, all facing east, built during 11th and 12th century.

Simhapura, the capital of Amaravati presently known as My Son is about 68 kilometres from Da Nang, surrounded by low mountains on three sides and a beautiful river bed on the fourth. Covered by dense forests My Son had been lost in oblivion after the decline of the Hindu Kingdom. In 1898 Mr. M.C. Paris rediscovered it followed by two French scientists, L. Finot and H. Parmentier.

One thing I noticed during my visits from Soaring Dragon Hanoi to its tail Ho Chi Minh City, visited hilly region of the North West to the highlands, Central Vietnam and various historical and modern cities of Vietnam that in its totality, a special picture of Vietnam emerges. Due endeavours are being undertaken to preserve and secure its historical heritage through construction of new memorials and temples so as to arouse a sense of pride among each and every citizen; so that the national identity and unity be the first and foremost for every citizen.

Be it the One Pillar Pagoda or the temples of My Son, Nha Trang or the history and ethnic museums of Da Nang, Hanoi, Ho Chi MInh City or the War Remnants Museums or the newly built Nguyen Thi Dinh and Nguyen Dinh Chien temples all present such a network of history and modernity that arouses a sense of belonging, common identity and unity among every citizen of the country.

4

CONFLUENCE OF TWO PERIODS : HANOI

My first encounter with Hanoi had been in the year 1982 when I had visited Vietnam in a goodwill mission under the leadership of Prof. Santimoy Ray, eminent historian of India and had stayed there for about five days.

Hoan Kiem Lake— in the Centre 'Turtle Tower' Pagoda, Hanoi

Whenever I am on any foreign tour, I have the habit of spending most of my time moving about roads and streets, meeting with the common people and interacting with them even without knowing their language. In Vietnam too, at times I also visited families at their shops and houses even without being invited, to know and understand the people and their culture. I am fortunate to have received hospitable treatment everywhere and this process continued from 1982 to 2017during my various visits to Vietnam especially Hanoi.

I may say that all these years I have become well acquainted with Hanoi, its roads, narrow lanes and by lanes, its most beautiful lakes, its shopping centres, where people from all over the globe visit for shopping, and where shopkeepers, particularly the women sell their wares through hard bargaining.

No, this metropolis is not a static one but has undergone lots of basic changes. Maintaining the old tradition the city roads, streets and thoroughfares have been widened. Wide footpaths provide ample space for pedestrians to move about comfortably. The area around every lake has been most impressively beautified to provide pleasure and enjoyment to hundreds of thousands of people, both local and tourists.

This city has a unique character of its own and that adds up its importance. For example, the unique confluence of art, culture, literature, trade, industry and politics that one finds here is rarely available in the world.

Hanoi, the capital of Vietnam, was called Thang Long imperial city under the Ly and Tran dynasties. The meaning of Thang Long is "City of the flying Dragon or soaring Dragon". The name Thang Long was given by King Ly Thai To(974 – 1028), who in 10th century moved the capital to the citadel of Dai La and changed the area's name to Thang Long. According to one legend King Ly Thai To saw a dragon rising into the air above his royal boat while he approached the site. From 1010 until 1802, it was the most important political centre of Vietnam. It was eclipsed by Hue, the imperial capital of Vietnam during the Nguyen Dynasty (1802-1945).

The name of Hanoi was bestowed in 1831 under the reign of the Nguyen emperor Minh Mang (1791-1891), the second king of the Nguyen dynasty. He renamed it Hanoi which means "Between Rivers" or "River Interior". Even when it became a mere former capital throughout the Nguyen Dynasty, it was the centre of immense activities for those who wanted to test their talents, will and luck. It served as the most important gateway to commerce, education and culture in the country. Strategically, this was an important area as it was right in the middle of the Red River Delta.

Hanoi was occupied by the French in 1883. During the French colonial period (1883–1945) the name Tonkin was used to refer to the entire region.

The city was occupied by the fascist Japanese in 1940 and liberated in 1945, when it briefly became the seat of the Viet Minh government after Ho Chi Minh proclaimed the independence of Vietnam. However, the French returned and reoccupied the city in 1946. After nine years of fighting between the French and Viet Minh forces, Viet Minh finally captured and won in Dien Bien Phu in 1954. Hanoi became the capital of an independent North Vietnam in 1954. In 1975 following the end of the war, Hanoi became the capital of a reunified Vietnam when North and South Vietnam were reunited.

Hanoi has witnessed numerous ups and downs during its history. In the year 1925 the intellectuals of the city had unitedly established a resistance front against the then French colonial rule and in due course of time it kept on expanding and changed or altered its name and form from time to time. Finally, the Communist Party of Vietnam took over its leadership and defeated the French colonialists as well as the US imperialists.

On X'mas of December 1956, the US Air Force attacked North Vietnam and Hanoi. The Vietnamese Army and Hanoi's armed forces retaliated most courageously shooting down 358 US Aircrafts. All through the 12 days from 18th to 29th December the US Air force had used B-52 bombers, modern F-111 jet fighters yet they were very badly defeated and this historic battle was called Dien Bien Phu in the Air.

In the original Dien Bien Phu battle in 1954, the French Army was decisively defeated and it was replaced by the US Army that stayed in Vietnam till 1975.

There is an interesting episode in 1956, during its indiscriminate bombings, the US Air force even bombed and destroyed a portion of the French Embassy, its ally as well. I had the occasion to witness the destroyed portion of the said Embassy. Even the famous One Pillar Pagoda of Hanoi was also raged to the ground and was subsequently rebuilt afresh in its original shape, after liberation.

Thus , Hanoi carries with it a rich legacy of a thousand years. Old tradition and culture throbs among a number of legends that are reflected in its various lively monuments.

Author at Ho Chi Minh Mausoleum with Ms. Kusum Jain and Ms. Pravamayee Samantaray at Ba Dih Sqnare, Hanoi.

Whenever I visit Hoan Kiem Lake, the Temple of Literature, old quarters of 36 narrow streets of Hanoi teeming with crowd, its buildings and traditional handicrafts shops, old citadel, One Pillar Pagoda, Ngo Son Temple and several such enchanting places, I find myself lost among the maze of the history and legends attached to this fascinating city.

Hanoi is known as the 'City of Lakes' and Hoan Kiem Lake is one of those lakes situated in the heart of the city and is the heart of Hanoi. To visit Hanoi as a tourist or visitor provides one with a mind blowing experience. On the first day of my first visit to this city, I remember having visited the Hoan Kiem Lake and its surroundings along with my fellow delegates. We were all

National Assembly Building of S.R. Vietnam, Hanoi.

enchanted by its beauty. There is a small stone Pagoda in its centre known as 'Turtle Tower' named after 'Return of the Sword' legend.

One such legend relates to Hoan Kiem Lake which means in English 'Lake of the Restored Sword'. This lake was once a part of the Red River. Through geographical changes that took place during thousand years, the lake moved eastward to its present position, a few kilometres away from the Red River. Earlier this lake was called Luc Thuy Lake or Green Water Lake since the water of the lake was green all through the year. Subsequently, in the 15th century it was named as Hoan Kiem Lake after the legend of Emperor Le Loi. According to the legend, during the war against the Minh aggressors, the Emperor was handed over a precious fairy sword by the Golden Turtle god. After a long struggle of ten years the emperor finally defeated the Chinese and reclaimed the nation's independence. After that, one day when the Emperor Le Loi was boating on the lake, a giant turtle appeared on its surface and approached towards the Emperor and said "now that peace has been restored to the nation, please return the sword to our god of waters". It immediately grabbed the sword with its mouth and submerged in the water of the lake.

The Emperor lamented the loss of such a valuable sword, yet he could neither find the sword nor the turtle. Finally, he consoled himself that his nation was free, so the sword needed to be returned. Hence he named the lake as Hoan Kiem Lake or Lake of the Restored Sword.

The Emperor Le Loi of the legend of Hoan Kiem Lake, his magical sword and the giant golden turtle all fasten me into an enchanting delusion whenever I visit Hoan Kiem Lake.

While passing through the Red Arch Bridge leading to Ngo Son Temple, an imaginary image of Emperor Le Thanh Tang emerges over my mental screen since he was the one who had built a pavilion over a hillock on Jade Island, where he used to visit with his friends on the fifteenth of every lunar month and used to write poems while sitting in the pavilion.

Recently on 17th June 2017 'Yoga Day' was celebrated as Yoga for Harmony & Peace, with much fanfare in Ly Thai To Park near Hoan Kiem Lake. It was due to the enthusiastic initiative of H. E. Mr. P. Harish, the Honourable Ambassador of Republic of India in Vietnam that thousands of Vietnamese yoga enthusiasts took part in it. Coincidentally myself and my colleague Kusum Jain, who were visiting Vietnam also participated in it on being invited by the Honourable Ambassador. I was amazed to note the craze among the Vietnamese about yoga.

Near Ly Thai To Park there is an Indira Gandhi Square where the bust of the Late Indian Prime Minister Indira Gandhi is installed. This square was named after Indira Gandhi after her assassination in 1984. Indira Gandhi had an emotional bond with Vietnam and addressed the then Vietnamese Premier H. E. Pham Van Dong as 'uncle' and shared quite cordial and intimate relations.

I have visited Ba Dinh Square of Hanoi a number of times. I am never tired of visiting this place. In fact, whenever I visit this place, I am thrilled. This was the place where President Ho Chi Minh had made a historic declaration of September 2nd 1945 – The Declaration of Independence of Democratic Republic of Vietnam among the massive presence of about 500,000 people, and the very first sentence of the declaration was "All men are created equal".

Ba Dinh Square also happens to be the place whenever I go there, I am overwhelmed with a sense of respect and admiration, for my icon, my ideal and charismatic peoples' hero Ho Chi Minh is lying here in eternal sleep at a grey granite and marble made grand mausoleum. In a pin drop silence, while passing by and seeing him through fibre glass, I read his inspiring words written inside the marble foyer "Nothing is precious than Independence and Freedom."

Behind the Mausoleum there is the residential quarter where Preisdent Ho Chi Minh had spent his last days and it displayed how austere life he led despite being the head of the nation since he always considered himself to be in the service of his people rather than a President of a nation. Next to the residential quarter is the famous pond where President Ho Chi Minh regularly fed the fishes, when he was in Hanoi. This indicated that he not only loved his people but his compassion was also for all the creatures. There are numerous trees in the compound, some of which were

Recently built 9 km long Nhat Tan Bridge, Hanoi.

planted by President Ho himself and he took its due care during his life time.

Next to the mausoleum is Ho Chi Minh Museum. Ho Chi Minh Museum displays many artifacts, and documents about the life and personality of Ho Chi Minh besides miniatures and various gifts gathered nationally and internationally. It was inaugurated on 19th May 1990 and has five extensive floors. The best way to visit the museum is to begin from up and then coming down. The museum has a square shape with an ethereal white lotus symbol. Four square blocks on the top floor is just a lotus flower. The whole museum has an elaborate description of Ho Chi Minh's life. All materials, photographs are displayed systematically and dynamically in order to help viewers to understand thoroughly and vividly the life and career of Ho Chi Minh. The Museum stores more than 12 thousand documents, artifacts, original films about the life and revolutionary career of President Ho Chi Minh. The museum presents the aspects of reinvented Vietnamese national heritage and helps to shape up a common national identity.

Just in front of the Mausoleum, on other side of the street is situated the National Assembly building that houses the Vietnamese

Parliament, the centre of Vietnamese politics. This new building of the National Assembly was built between 2009 and 2014. It acts as a bridge between the Vietnamese past and its future. This building has been erected at the site of former People's Building in the area known as the Citadel, opposite Ho Chi Minh Mausoleum and houses the Plenary Chamber and the Representatives' Offices, of 493 representatives from 58 provinces. The National Assembly building of Vietnam is a magnificent piece of architecture and creates a bridge between the Vietnamese past and the country's future. It is constructed in Hanoi's historic city centre, at the site of the former People's Building in the area known as the Citadel, opposite the Ho Chi Minh Mausoleum. I believe, it was not a mere coincidence. It was built possibly to keep reminding the law makers about the legacy of Ho Chi Minh and to follow his people oriented socialist philosophy while formulating policies and planning.

Ceramic artisans at work in a workshop at Ba Trang pottery village, Hanoi

I may never be able to forget the evening of 13th June, 2017 as we had the honour of meeting H. E. Mrs. Nguyen Thi Kim Ngan, the honourable Chairperson of the National Assembly. Madam Ngan is one among the four most high ranking leaders of Vietnam besides being the first woman chairperson of Vietnam's National Assembly. We were, in fact, hypnotized by her humility, balanced, soft and firm voice.

After our half an hour long meeting, while we were preparing to depart, she gifted us a signed photograph of our meeting. The snap was taken during the meeting. It was such a lovely gift that we would cherish throughout our life.

I am filled with a sense of reverence whenever I visit the Temple of Literature, the old monument of Hanoi, as the emperor Lý Thánh Tông, highly valued the scholars, even more than the kings, and respected them. The king had named it 'Temple of Literature' instead of Maths or Philosophy, as in the ancient time Literature was meant to denote all the learnings following the Confucian education system. The Temple of Literature is the first University of Vietnam dedicated to Confucius. This historic temple pays its tribute to the great philosopher, as also to many scholars and intellectuals, who have contributed towards building Vietnam's scholarly culture. The temple was built in 1070 during the Ly Dynasty and since then Hanoi has become the centre of education. When it was first established, only people of noble birth were admitted. In 1442 the University opened its doors to receive talented students from across the country.

Even in the French colonial period, as the capital of the Indochina Federation, Hanoi was the educational centre of the Indochina region where the French set up vocational schools and colleges, including Indochina University and Indochina Medical University, which later became the foundation for Vietnamese higher education.

Hanoi is still the largest educational centre of Vietnam, where there are over 50 universities and many colleges training human resources for different important sectors. There are well-known universities, such as Hanoi Medical University, Vietnam National University, Hanoi, Hanoi University of Technology, Hanoi Architectural University, Military Engineering Academy, Foreign Trade University, Vietnam University of Fine Arts, National Economics University, Hanoi, Teachers Training University, the University of Civil Engineering, etc. These are the leading multi-disciplinary and specialized universities in Vietnam.

One Pillar Pagoda is one of the oldest monuments in Hanoi. It was built in 1049 by the Emperor Ly Thanh Tong when he was blessed with a son. He had built it as an expression of his gratitude towards goddess Quan Am.

There are numerous other Pagodas and temples that bring into memory the centuries old history of the city. This City Hanoi had witnessed a number of ups and downs, feudal, imperial and colonial phases and today it is standing on the solid base of socialism.

Hanoi is also known for its beautiful lakes. In fact, Hanoi is located on a typical alluvial plain, where seasonal flooding has deposited river sediment over thousands of years. These deposits have formed the river steps, elevated areas between which are lower areas filled with scattered lakes and swamps that are the traces of the ancient river beds. The lakes, are free of any encroachment and most well preserved. Hanoi has numerous lakes that are the remnants of the ancient rivers that once flowed through it. In the proper city West Lake, Truc Bach Lake and Hoan Kiem Lake or the Sword Lake are the most important symbols of Hanoi's landscape and culture. Other famous lakes in the inner city include Thien Quang and Thu Le Lakes. There are also many other large lakes such as the lakes of Kim Lien, Linh Dam, Ngai Son Dong Mo, Suoi Hai, Meo Gu, Xuan Khanh, Tuy Lai and Quan Son, Truc Bach Lake etc.

In the numerous narrow lanes and by lanes of Hanoi there are thousands of shops that sell almost all the necessary goods for the consumers. In the open space around the Hoan Kiem Lake also there are hundreds of shops in the close vicinity that cater to the foreign tourists and most of the shops are looked after by the women shopkeepers, who have sky rocketing bargaining skill.

Since hundreds of years West Lake forms a prominent part in the landscape of Hanoi. The Kings of Ly and Tran Dynasties built several palaces around the lake for relaxation and amusement. The area of the lake is over 500 hectares. The road around the lake is 17 km long and includes the segments of the Red River Dyke. Geological studies have proved that this lake was once an ancient part of the Red River before it changed to its present course. During one of my visits, I had walked around the lake in an evening and had enjoyed watching people walking, children playing.

People enjoy their time out around numerous lakes that the city provides for relaxation and amusement. They enjoy their walk around these lakes with ice cream, coffee and shopping of various types of small souvenirs and gift items that are being vended around the lakes. Grand parents come for walk with their grand children some times in pram, or holding the fingers of the children to make them play.

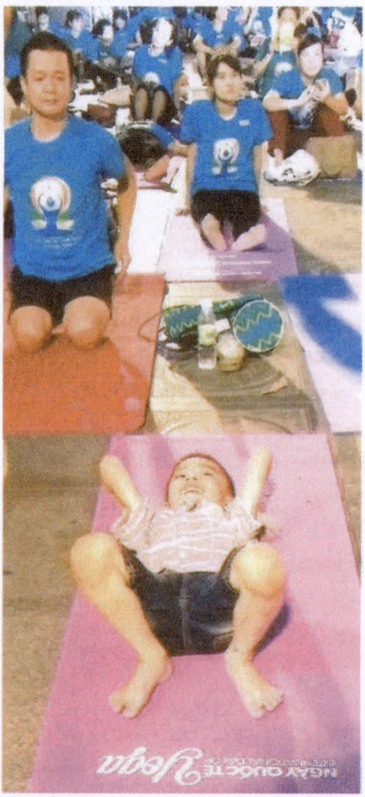

A Vietnamese Child Yoga enthusiast performing a yoga posture on International Yoga Day on 17th June 2017 at Ly Thai To Park near Hoan Kiem Lake.

In few of my visits I had the occasion to go to Water Puppetry Theatre which is a Traditional Folk Art, very popular among the tourists these days. Water puppetry is a distinct Vietnamese art which had its origins in the 12th century. In water puppetry, a split-bamboo screen obscures puppets which stand in water and are manipulated using long poles hidden beneath the water. Epic and folktales storylines are played out with many different characters, often depicting traditional scenes of Vietnamese life.

Around ten Kilometres away from Hanoi is a village Bat Trang, traditionally very rich in its pottery industry, having a history of seven centuries. There are hundreds of pottery shops where one

The Author with H.E. Mr. P. Harish, Ambassador of India in Vietnam on International Yoga Day at Ly Thai To Park, Hanoi on 17th June 2017.

may see the artisans shaping up various pottery items, colouring them with exquisite colours and according to one's pocket one may purchase the beautiful pieces to one's fancy. It is located in an area rich in clay, the village has advantage of ingredients to create fine ceramics. Moreover, lying besides the Red river, between Thang Long and Pho Hien, two ancient trade centres in the north of Vietnam during 15th-17thcentury, Bat Trang's ceramics were favourite products not only in domestic market, but also foreign ones thanks to Japan, Chinese and Western trading boats that passed by.

Since 1986, as a strategy of economic reforms and development, more attention has been vested in the village and the world gets a chance to know more about Vietnamese porcelain through many high quality exported Bat Trang's ceramic products.

There is a modernized traditional 'Van Phuc Silk Village' on the lines of 'pottery village' about 10km southwest of Hanoi Old Quarter, It is renowned for its traditional weaving and premium quality silk products. Keeping the basic character of a village new facilities are added to attract the tourists like roadside eateries, tea-coffee stalls, stalls for sugarcane juice etc. There are around 200 families that reside in the 'Silk Village'. It is proud to be the most ancient silk village which provides the best silk in Vietnam. Nowadays, although the weaving has been mechanized for higher productivity, there are still simple manual looms in some houses in the village which help tourists contemplate the genuinely traditional Vietnamese way of making silk.

The night market of Hanoi is special attraction for the shoppers. It is said that here one may have a variety of items from a needle to an elephant. Around eight in the night one may find hundreds of shops selling various wares on the roadside and these shops do brisk business till midnight. After six in the morning and before seven in the evening you will not find any trace of those hundreds of shops that were doing brisk business between eight and twelve in the night.

Hanoi is one thousand years old. Very recently the city had celebrated its 1000th Anniversary of foundation with great fanfare in the year 2010 and thousands of people from all over the world had participated in the said celebration. Although Hanoi is now a most modern metropolis with numerous high-rise buildings, skyscrapers and multitudes of inhabitants, it has still retained many values of its unique traditional culture.

It was a pleasant surprise for me to visit 'Centre of Indian Studies' at Ho Chi Minh National Academy of Politics where we had an interactive meeting with Prof Le Van Toan , Director and Dr. Nguyen Thi Phuong Thao, Deputy Director of the Centre. It is the first overseas research center specializing in India and working like India Information Centre. The Centre, today, is dedicatedly and actively engaged in promoting relations through culture and literature and has become a strong and reliable bridge between Vietnam and India. It plans to publish six to eight books on India in a year. It also is planning to publish one magazine very soon. Apart from organizing International conferences, the centre has translated many works of eminent Indian writers from English to Vietnamese language. It is my honour and privilege that my book "Vietnam Liberation War: Role of Calcutta" has also been translated in Vietnamese language and the first edition has already been soldout. It has a library also. The Centre was inaugurated by the then Indian President Pranab Mukherjee on Sept 15, 2014.

Every visit to this city surprises me with some new additions. In 2015, while going from the airport to the city, while crossing the Red river, I had passed through a long newly built bridge. I was literally charmed by its beautiful construction. My host from Vietnam Writers' Association Ms. Dao Kim Hoa proudly told me that the Nhat Tan Bridge, was the seventh bridge, 9 kilometers long with five suspension towers having six lanes superhighway. It was an engineering marvel of the city.

In 1982 when I had visited Hanoi for the first time, there was not a single five-star hotel, whereas in 2017 there were about twenty five-star hotels besides hundreds of hotels of various standards suiting to the pockets of tourists of various categories. Besides hotels there are numerous massage parlours and bath centres on every nook and corner of the city and some indulge in flesh trade even under camouflage to make quick money.

Carrying forward the historical legacy Hanoi is presently engaged in ever new constructions of bridges, roads, five star hotels, new sky scrapers, offices and infrastructure. Eco-park complex, life style shops, coffee shops, restaurants and all these present

Newly developed Urban Housing Complex at Eco Park, Hanoi

multicoloured images of modern Hanoi.

Today it is a tourist delight for it provides a number of shopping options to the tourists. Besides various traditional shopping centres, a number of big malls have come up where besides shopping one may have a number of entertainment and amusement options. One such big mall is 68 Storeyed Lotte Mall, 72 storeyed Landmark Building where departmental stores, and commercial offices are there. Presently the work of underground railway – Metro, is also in progress both in Hanoi and Ho Chi Minh City and may be by the end of this year a big section of it may be commissioned for the benefit of the passengers.

Nowadays this thousand years' old capital city displays itself with a new look. Over a decade ago, it was hard to imagine that Hanoi would have a fast and rigorous development as today. In suburban areas many new modern urban centres are being developed called miniature European towns like Vinhomes Royal City, Vinhomes Times City, Vinhomes Riverside etc. Special importance is being given to the development of Municipal Green space with one million trees and 25 Public Parks in coming five years.

In June 2017 on my way back to Bat Trang pottery village, I visited Eco Park. To my utter surprise, it was not like earlier Eco tourism parks that I had visited during my visit to Hue near Terracotta Museum and in Thai Nguyen city near man made Nui Coc Lake.

It is an urban township of residential flats in multi storied complex and Villas have been constructed on the outskirts of Hanoi for peaceful pollution free living. The Villas are quite costly and only rich Hanoians can afford but the flats are in affordable range of the middle class. There are schools, kindergarten schools, shops, markets, restaurants, play gardens but all are quiet. Streets and gardens are empty. The whole area is surrounded by varieties of full grown up trees and plants so densely that it seems like a forest. The Eco Park is still under development. The first phase is nearly complete. Houses and Villas are presently unoccupied and waiting for the people to come and live there. It is a futuristic dream project of 21st Century Hanoi.

Present day Hanoi may be compared with any developed city or metropolis of Europe. It is a lively, vibrant and lovely fast developing city with hospitable people.

5

DAZZLING CITY DA NANG

It was December 1982 when on our way from Hanoi to Ho Chi Minh City we had reached Da Nang, a small village like town situated on the banks of River Han. In fact, it was a fishermen's village, where excepting a few buildings erected by the French Government, rest were all shanties, hutments and stilt houses. In

Mothers' Memorial, Da Nang.

the name of transport we could locate only few bicycles, rickshaws and a few hundred motor-bikes and countable cars. One could witness the remains of colossal devastation that Vietnam had undergone on every foot-step. Buildings, roads, footpaths, and one river bridge, all were in most pitiable condition. In absence of a bridge people of Da Nang had to use country boats to cross the river to reach the other side of the city.

While roaming about in the city we strayed towards some agricultural fields, where we met Indian agronomists, who were sent from Agriculture College, Roorkee by the Government of India to impart agricultural training to the Vietnamese cultivators. They were engaged in training the Vietnamese farmers the ways and means to grow more food crops by improving the fertility and quality of the soil. It was a pleasant surprise for us.

When confronted with authorities and the common Vietnamese, however, they were least apprehensive. On the contrary they remarked with a sense of conviction that they were not at all ashamed of their poverty, as it was imposed upon them. They seemed rather pleased in sharing the poverty among themselves and had immense self-belief that the day was not far when they would overcome the conditions of poverty and would succeed in national reconstruction of Vietnam into a developing nation. I came across the similar remark in Hanoi as well, which indicated that it represented the thinking of the nation as a whole.

In this process of nation building they firmly believed that their great leader Ho Chi Minh was with them and kept inspiring and encouraging them in their endeavours. (Ho Chi Minh had expired in 1969). Their inordinate self confidence did not at all seem to me as an overstatement.

Since then I had the occasion of visiting Da Nang for about five times and every time I was pleasantly surprised to see its transformation. Da Nang was changing and that too with a fast pace. In fact it was changing every day.

My visit to Da Nang in August 2017 was quite amazing for me as I failed to locate the Da Nang of 1982.

The erstwhile fishermen's village had turned into a modern city that could be compared with any world class city. Today, Da Nang has developed on both the sides of Han River. Both the banks of river Han in Da Nang have been developed into beautiful tourist spots and the natural beauty of about ten kilometre long sea beach only adds to its beauty.

The remodelling and reconstruction work of Da Nang had started in 1997 and within a short span of 20 years it has transformed into a world class tourist spot. Its earlier inhabitants still remember that prior to 1997 Da Nang was a small city with most ordinary and simple system of roads and housing. There were only sandy pathways in fishing villages besides untidy, temporary stilt houses along the river. Today the past images have disappeared and a most modern township with all the facilities and comforts one looks for, has emerged. Shanty and stilt houses and also the poor fishing villages no more exist and have been replaced by a long road along the Da Nang Bay.

Earlier there was a dilapidated bridge on the river Han while now there are about nine bridges that have their respective elegance and beauty. The latest built Dragon Bridge is a marvel and quite captivating in its lighting arrangement. On every weekend thousands of tourists and locals assemble in the vicinity of the bridge to watch the fire emitting dragon while enjoying sips of their coffee or drinks.

Once the bicycles were the common mode of transport in Da Nang, while today, it has been replaced by Motorbikes. Almost every adult today has his/her motorbike. Rickshaws have been replaced by cars and those in usage are for the joy rides of the tourists. Public transport viz. the buses and the taxis are all air-conditioned and comfortable.

There are wide network of hundreds of hotels, Guest Houses one

The Han River Bridge- Pride of the People of Da Nang.

to five star hotels and resorts that are available to the tourists with most modern amenities and the charges range from 10 USD to 100 USD.

Da Nang is one of the five largest cities of Vietnam having a land area of about 1255.5 sq. km., a population of about one million and an archipelago on the East Sea. It is situated in the centre of Vietnam, 764 kms. from Hanoi and 964 kms. from Ho Chi Minh City. It lies on the north-south transport axis of land, rail, sea and air routes. With its advantageous geographical location Da Nang plays a very important role in Central Vietnam.

On its most ambitious journey towards development during last two decades it has accomplished miraculous achievements. The city centre, was planned for development from the centre towards the West, North West, South and South East and as a result Da Nang is much more larger and different than in the past. It has expanded many times and upgraded its infrastructure, thereby presenting a completely changed portrait of the city. In fact Da Nang has developed with a more rapid pace than any other city of Vietnam. Within a shortest span of two decades or even less, it has turned from most underdeveloped 'fishermen's village' to a well developed world-class city.

Da Nang is a young, dynamic and developing city where due care is taken to protect the environment. Before issuing license for any economic project, the city authorities carefully scrutinize its environmental impact. In fact, the authorities and people of Da Nang are most conscious and aware of protecting the environment. One may hardly encounter the scene of people dumping garbage and rubbish on streets and public places. One may not find stray animals anywhere on road.

It is not only a city for tourists having immense tourist attractions but it is equally a prominent trading centre of Vietnam having enormous potential for trading and industrial activities. Besides various local manufacturing units it also has numerous industrial units and offices of well known Multinational Corporations and has nine Industrial Zones. Despite all these there still are enormous opportunities and possibilities to be explored by the entrepreneurs.

Administration in Da Nang is business friendly and so is the attitude of the labour which is quite positive. Da Nang has most favourable business friendly environment in Central Vietnam. It was ranked number one in the provincial competitiveness index in three consecutive years (2008-2010). Da Nang Port is the Eastern gateway to the East-West Economic Corridor (EWEC). EWEC is 1450 km route linking Indian and Pacific Oceans. From Myanmar, it runs across 13 provinces of four countries of GMS to Da Nang Port as the end point.

Da Nang has made ever new experiments with the artistic architectural designing in its architecture and that is why its architectural marvels are so highly appreciated by the tourists. It is the artistic and imaginative thinking of the architects that they have designed the huge exhibition centre of Da Nang giving it the shape of wings of a flying bird. Some of the other architectural marvels of Da Nang are the Martyrs' Memorial built in the memory of martyrs, who sacrificed their lives for their country; the huge statue of the affectionate mother, who had given birth to heroic and brave sons; giant wheel on the lines of 'London Eye' that may be termed as 'Da Nang Eye' and numerous beautiful sculptures of various shapes and sizes that adorn both the banks of river Han are quite capable of creating a charming impact over the tourists.

Besides, all the bridges that are built over river Han are the specimen of excellent architectural marvels and each bridge has its own distinguishing features. Today it is termed as the city of bridges. It has about nine bridges and every bridge does not only serve the traffic purpose but also breathes life into the city by ensuring equitable development on both the banks of River Han since the bridges crossing over the river have shortened the distance between the two river banks and have thereby provided an easy access on both the river banks. At night all the bridges are lighted with various sparkling lights that turn Da Nang into a dazzling, colourful and legendary city unlike any other city in Vietnam.

There are four 'Super Bridges' that infuse life and breath to Da Nang and symbolize the power of the city. Those bridges are – the Han River Bridge, The Thuan Phuoc Bridge, The Tran Thi Ly Bridge and the Dragon Bridge. There are few more bridges in Da Nang viz. Nguyen Van Troi Bridge, Nguyen Tri Phuong Bridge, Tien Son Bridge, Hoa Xuan Bridge and Cam Le Bridge.

The Han River Bridge has a glorious past. This bridge is the first one that was designed by the Vietnamese architects and the workers. It is the first suspension bridge in Da Nang that connected the west and east sides of the city. This bridge that happens to be one of the marvels of the planned development is also termed as the pride of Da Nang's people since this unique rotating bridge was built by the local authorities with the local people's contribution to fulfil their long standing desire. The foundation of this bridge was laid on 2nd September 1998 and it was completed and inaugurated in a record time on 29th March 2000 on the occasion of the 25th anniversary of city's liberation. The length of the Han River Bridge is 487.8 meters;

Children enjoying their day out on Da Nang sea beach.

the width is 12.9 meters including 11 spans; the length of each span being 33 metres. The beams and the main tower of the bridge were built of steel while the surface was built of reinforced concrete.

Once, the other side of the bank of Han River was just a place that had houses and agricultural fields. Today both the banks of the river Han have been so beautifully and enchantingly decorated that a tourist may be lured to spend hours after hours over sips of green tea, coffee or coconut water and rejuvenate and reenergize himself. It would be relevant to mention here that Vietnam is quite popular for its coffee culture and with every cup of coffee, green tea is available for free. Be it an urban area or a distant hamlet, everywhere there is a wide network of coffee-houses and Da Nang is no exception to it. One such café cum shop is Da Nang souvenirs and Café on the bank of Han River and near Novotel hotel. It is modern and relaxing ambience with good service. It offers Vietnamese Coffee, Cafe Latte, smoothies, cakes and ice creams of different varieties. There are varieties of beautiful Vietnamese handicrafts and souvenirs displayed for sale.

On the Paris pattern, roadside restaurants have its own attraction and craze in Da Nang. While relishing the sips of coffee one may enjoy the sight of people passing by for hours. Apart from restaurants and coffee shops, chain of hotels including five star hotels is seen standing on the bank of the other side of Han River. Sea beach has also been developed in such a fashion that one may enjoy the ambience of a country side along with the most modern amenities. Hutment shaped hotels and restaurants are plenty in numbers but maintaining sufficient space in between to retain the cleanliness. Even in the midst of the rush of thousands of tourists, what to talk of garbage dump it is hard to find rubbish littered anywhere. The cleaning staff is constantly engaged in keeping their respective areas clean. On the sea beach there are sufficient numbers of both expensive and not so expensive hotels.

There is a hillock named Son Tra Mountain about 4-5 kms. from the city. Until ten years from now i.e. till 2007 this area was a desolate hillock covered with greenery when a Buddhist monk located this area and thought to develop it into an attractive spiritual centre for the tourists keeping its natural beauty intact. He visualized of installing a 67 feet high idol of Lord Buddha on the summit of the hillock. The diameter of the idol should be 37 mtr., he thought and got engaged in giving a proper shape to his imagination. The Government provided necessary land for the project and the construction began with the economic aid received from immigrant Vietnamese scattered all over the world.

A charming View of a Da Nang sea beach.

Today, the area has developed into a small township that is regularly visited by thousands of tourists who enjoy their stay. There is a Buddhist Monastery, a Buddha Temple, a Guest house, a small shopping centre, a museum besides arrangement for tea, coffee, snacks and refreshments.

About 15 kms. from Da Nang City there are Marble Mountains that were once called Champa Parvat. Marble Mountains and Hai Van Pass or the Passage of Clouds are the major tourist attraction of Da Nang City that are visited by more than a million tourists every year. Thuy Son Mountain or The Mountain of Water is the

Panoramic View of Da Nang City.

principal highlight of the visit. To get to the top of the Mountain of Water of the Marble Mountains group one has to use two paths formed by flights of stairs. The path on the western side of the mountain is composed of 156 steps and the path on the eastern side has about 108 steps. Since 2011, however, for the convenience of the tourists an elevator is also installed.

The interiors of the Marble Mountains are full of marbles and for more than 400 years mining of the marble to make furniture, sculptures, jewellery and for building purposes, was customary. The quality of the marble extracted from these mountains was so superior that Ho Chi Minh Mausoleum in Hanoi was decorated by the marble from these mountains. To avoid further damage and over exploitation of these mountains, presently the mining of marble from these mountains is no more allowed and the marble is imported from Ninh Binh and other provinces.

The Central Part of Da Nang City looks stunningly beautiful and adorned like a bride after dusk when a number of arches decorated by colourful bulbs spread light soothing to the eyes all around; when trees and plants look far more green and pleasing to the eyes. Various small and big sculptures adoring the bank of the river look even more beautiful. At night the area looks brilliantly glittering in the light of the coloured bulbs. During weekend numerous performances of music make it quite identical to a fairyland. I had the occasion to visit various cities in Asia and Europe but never came across such a beautiful sight that provides a unique experience to relish.

Da Nang fascinates me for various reasons and the foremost being that it shares about two thousand years' old cultural link with India. Once it was a part of the Hindu Kingdom in Vietnam. So, whenever I visit Da Nang, I feel nostalgic besides feeling at home.

What is even more important for me is that whenever I have been to Da Nang, I have received the love and affection of the people in abundance, beginning from the Chairman and Vice Chairman of its People's Committee to the Chairman of Da Nang Association of Friendship Organizations to the common people.

Another worth mentioning reason for my fascination is the miraculous transformation of this city from a fishermen's village to a world class city besides its beautiful landscape. In fact, all these distinguishing features had motivated and prompted me to write the book titled 'Da Nang: City of Wonders'. This book was released under the joint auspices of the Chairman of DAFO and the Vice Chairman of Da

Nang Writers Association on 24th August 2017 wherein myself and my colleague Kusum Jain had the honour of being invited.

Da Nang is not only a tourist centre or an industrial hub but it is also a distinguished place in the field of art, culture and literature. More than a hundred writers, poets, journalists and artists belonging to various age groups had participated in the book-release ceremony. Some of the writers had played an active role in the freedom struggle of Vietnam.

We were told that a sizable population of Da Nang belonged to the Poets' fraternity. It has a powerful Writers' Union that has a building of its own where writers meet, interact and hold various functions.

To mark the occasion of release of my book titled 'Da Nang : City of Wonders' the Da Nang Association of Friendship Unions and Vietnam India Friendship Association, Da Nang had invited me and six of my colleagues of Indo-Vietnam Solidarity Committee, West Bengal to Da Nang in August 2017. The book was released at a solemn function at the Conference Hall of Da Nang Writers' Association (DWA) in the august presence of Mr. Khiem, the President of DWA and Mr. Truong, the Chairman of DAFO, Mr. Vo Van Thang, the President of VIFA, Da Nang. Writers, poets, intellectuals and artists of the city belonging to various age-groups were present on the occasion in a good number.

As had already been mentioned in various earlier chapters, the writers and poets fraternity in Vietnam had not only participated in resistance and liberation war but had played a still greater role in creation of a new society on socialist thinking, which had been the most challenging task at that time and the writers of Da Nang also were no exception to it. They fought the war with the might of pen as well as gun. Even today the writers are equally converged about the problems of the society viz. corruption, increasing disparity, environment etc., and are fearlessly focusing their writings over these main concerns.

We stayed in Da Nang for about five days during our stay despite our most hectic schedule whenever we got some leisure time, we wandered around the city and saw for ourselves that the development on massive scale had taken place in the city. A new residential 39 storeyed Blooming Tower A has recently been completed. Another Sobil Da Nang Tower 1 is expected to be completed in 2018. Many new sky-scrappers have also been constructed on both the sides of River Han, thereby changing the face of Da Nang. The most impressive building recently constructed is the 34 storeyed Da Nang Administrative building, where we had the honour of meeting H.E. Mr. Tran Van Mien, the Vice Chairman of Da Nang Peoples' Committee.

This time apart from shopping at Han Market built by the French in 1940, I went to 'Big C' market, Con Market, known as Da Nang Commercial Centre. The prices at 'Big C' is fixed while in Han and Con Market I haggled a lot to buy. The other shopping malls offering entertainment are Lotte Mart Da Nang and Vinh Trung Plaza.

Today, Da Nang is growing rapidly and growth is its prime recourse. Day by day Da Nang is becoming a more and more charming and fascinating city. One is free to visit Da Nang to see this miracle with one's own eyes.

I may sound a bit biased but when it comes to talking about Da Nang, I may only say it is bold and beautiful, it is a lovely and loving city with the people who love and care for their guests, who are courteous, sensitive and emotional. When we were departing from Da Nang, the Chairman of DAFO and the committed members of DAFO, Mr. Tuyen Nguyen accompanied us to the airport to bid us a 'good bye'. We were so charged emotionally that practically we had tears in our eyes. It had a deep impact on me and I may never be able to forget it.

Whenever, I visit Da Nang, I feel at home and when I return to my home town Kolkata, I still miss the city and the people of Da Nang a lot.

6

FINANCIAL CAPITAL HO CHI MINH CITY

I am so fascinated of Ho Chi Minh City (formerly Saigon) that it has always been the first or last leg of my various visits to Vietnam. In fact, I have always relished spending some of my time sitting near the grand statue of President Ho Chi Minh at the Ho Chi Minh Square in District 1 overlooking the crowd passing by. Despite the area bustling with activities and teeming with the people I find peace and solace near the statue of Uncle Ho.

Students of a local school posing for a pholograph near Ho Chi Minh statue in front of People's Committee City Hall Building at Nguyen Hue Walking Boulevard.

Walking down the street from Ho Chi Minh Square and enjoying the sight around within no time I reach at the bank of river Saigon. While sitting at a nearby bench suddenly the historical moment of 106 years back emerges before eyes when a 21 years old young boy Nguyen Tat Thanh had boarded Admiral Latouch Treville ship in the guise of a cook and had started his journey to some unknown destination to find ways and means to liberate his country on 5th

June 1911. On the bank of this very Saigon river the said young man had said "good bye, we will meet again" with tearful eyes to his lady love, least knowing that they may never meet again. The same very young man was later known as the great leader Ho Chi Minh. Thirty years later in 1941 Nguyen Tat Thanh did return to his homeland Vietnam but could never return to Saigon.

Ho Chi Minh Square is, in fact, heart of the city that houses the grand light yellow coloured colonial building of the People's Committee City Hall, which is a unique specimen of French architecture. This building was designed by French architect Gardes on the lines of Hotel De Ville, Paris and the building was completed in about ten years. Today it is the political nerve centre of Ho Chi Minh City and it houses various government offices besides offices of various ministers where common entry is restricted.

On one side of the Ho Chi Minh Square there is the historic Rex Hotel that was built by the French in 1927. The roof-top Bar of this hotel was quite popular during Vietnam war when military officials, diplomats, war correspondents etc. used to have their cocktails and dinners here. It is said that the bar and the food served in this hotel is one of the best in the world. I remember, the then Chairman of the People's Committee of Ho Chi Minh City Mr. Huynh Dam had invited me and my colleague Kusum Jain over Lunch and it was here that for the first time I had relished the popular Hotpot Soup of Vietnam.

At a walking distance from Ho Chi Minh Square there is the oldest and biggest Ben Thanh Market where one may have anything and everything from needle to elephant. This market was established by the French in 1859. In 1870, however, it was destroyed by fire and was rebuilt by 1912 and in 1985 it was further renovated. This market has a unique character of its own. There are hundereds of small shops managed by the women shopkeepers, who are hard bargainers and it depends on the customer's skill to bargain with them. Beginning from fruits, vegetables, spices, biscuits, chocolates, toffees, coffee, tea, apparels, textile, suitcases, bags, umbrellas, shoes, sandals, garments, under-garments, handicrafts, imitation jewellery and all types of consumer items of various brands are available in the market. On one side of the market there are numerous food and cuisine stalls where one may find people enjoying food of their tastes and choices.

Ho Chi Minh city is the youngest city of Vietnam. It is about three hundred years old , eight years younger than our city Kolkata. HCM city was established in 1698. Mr. Nguyen Huu Canh (1650-1700), a high ranking general of Lord Nguyen Phuc Chu, set up Gia Dinh province and established the first southern administration, marking birth of the city. After reclaiming the land in 1802, Canh drew up programme for forming villages, restoring social order, formulating civil code setting up legal system and determining territorial borders. Saigon-Gia Dinh became the economic and commercial centre of South due to its social and geographical position. It became the gateway of the region and the world. In 1859, the French had occupied Saigon and the southern region and had declared it as their colony. They then tried to turn Saigon into the 'Pearl of the Far East' with a view to boost their colonial power and policies. The French invested in the fields that were beneficial to their homeland. They maintained and established monopolies of salt, liquor and opium.

Since 1930, workers, farmers and people of South and Saigon participated intensely in various revolutionary activities, guerrilla warfare against colonial and imperial power, leading the success of August Revolution in 1945. It was unfortunate that French invaders occupied Saigon again and whole of the Southern region and established autonomous Southern region with a Puppet Government, thus dividing Vietnam in North and South Vietnam. Entire country fought for its national independence and reunification and finally got unified after 30 years of resistance war against the French and Americans. On 30th April 1975, Saigon and the entire southern region was liberated and Vietnam was unified after years of resistance war against the French and the American invaders. Unfortunately, however, President Ho Chi

Subramaniam Swamy Temple at Ho Chi Minh City.

Minh was no more there to see the unified Vietnam. He had died in 1969.

After reunification the National Assembly of Vietnam decided to rechristen Saigon-Cholon Gia Dinh as Ho Chi Minh City, paying a worthwhile tribute to the great leader President Ho.

Since 17th century it had already started bustling with trade and other economic activities due to its strategic location. The city lies along the Saigon River to the north of the Mekong River delta and about 80 km from the South China Sea. Today, due to its locational advantage and being the largest city, it is a focal economic hub and financial capital of Vietnam. It is one of the biggest venues to attract foreign direct investment. It had great potential for industry, export, tourism and services forming an agro-industrial economic base. Today it is being transformed from resource base to a brain-power economy.

In 1982 the last leg of our journey, that had started from Hanoi was Ho Chi Minh City. Even during those days, this city was far more developed than any other city of Vietnam, including the Capital city Hanoi. During the period of liberation war between 1945 and 1975, when almost whole of Vietnam had suffered a great devastation, Ho Chi Minh City escaped it as it had been serving as the capital city of the puppet regime of the South

Vietnam established by the French and the U.S. It served as the biggest military base for the foreign aggressors, and so it escaped the carpet bombing. Of course, the areas nearby suffered a great devastation as the freedom fighters were launching concerted attacks on the US army positions.

Even during those days Saigon had maximum number of motorbikes as compared to any other Vietnamese city. Even the numbers of cars in Saigon during those days might have been around four to five thousand, although the principal mode of transportation was cycles and cycle rickshaws.

Despite this development, the city suffered to a certain extent under poverty, especially in and adjoining areas of the city near the river bank where there had been few slums and which contributed a lot towards the pollution of the river, and where dilapidated buildings, narrow lanes and even narrower by-lanes and beggars were common features.

Sixty eight storeyed high rise building Bitexco Financeal Tower built in 2010 at Nguyen Hue Street in Ho Chi Minh City overlooking Saigon River in the background.

A few years back one of my Vietnamese friend had told me that Vietnam was changing every day. During my several visits I witnessed the truth behind my friend's observation. For instance, keeping almost in tact the basic character of the old Ho Chi Minh City, many new multi-storeyed office buildings, Shopping Malls, book – shops, Hotels, Art galleries, Movie theatres, bars, restaurants have been built. A great deal of entertainment keeps you awake all through night in Disrict 1. The river Saigon that presented a shabby look in 1982 for there were several slums on its shore, has now been beautified with wide footpaths along with tree plantation in a big way. In between the footpath there are numerous parks full of flowers and decorated with lights. Of course benches are there where one could sit and enjoy the scenic beauty and relax. There are also small kiosks of eatables where one may enjoy the culinary delicacies of Vietnamese food.

During my visit in 2017, I visited District 7 which is being developed as the future face of Ho Chi Minh city. It has been planned to be a Western District serving high quality villas, high living standard apartments have been constructed. Fast food restaurants, coffee shops, bars have been opened besides KFC, Lotteria. Recently Domino Pizza just opened its first franchise in Vietnam in this District 7.

There are 24 Districts in Ho Chi Minh Province and all the districts are developing with fast pace. Malls, villas, high class apartments, high rise buildings and infrastructures are being developed.

During my several visits I noticed with astonishment the changing horizon of Vietnam. High-rise buildings, bridges, flyovers, metallic roads, new pagodas, new temples and memorials were coming up in almost every province. It seemed as though Vietnam was in a construction mode and determined to develop its basic infrastructure.

I had visited Ho Chi Minh City earlier a number of times but in 2017 I could not recognize it, particularly its Nguyen Hue flower Street, which has almost changed its character. In 2015 a monumental statue of Ho Chi Minh has been stalled in the Ho Chi minh square and there is a wide walking strip in the middle of the road from the Headquarters of the People's Committee City Hall to the Saigon River. The long stretch has been built and beautified on both sides with the lush green trees. On one end of Nguyen Hue Street there is Ho Chi Minh Square while on the other flows the river Saigon. Earlier the street was in the centre while on both sides of it there were rows of trees and behind which there were hotels of various categories besides offices, restaurants, malls, coffee shops etc. Now, the street has a walking stretch in the centre with wide street on its both the sides through which the traffic continues to ply.

The entire face lift of Nguyen Hue Street was beyond my imagination. The new changed look was so beautiful that it has become an ideal destination not only for the people of Saigon but for tourists also. Earlier when my friends talked about Ho chi minh City, it was usually about the highest Bitexco building, Peoples Committee City Hall building, Ben Thanh Market, or the Notre Dame Cathedral, but now the Nguyen Hue Walking street has become the hottest attraction of the city.

While strolling on the walking street, I saw some leisurely people sitting on the side benches, some were walking, talking, laughing and taking selfies and also some were dating. Since evening to dawn, the fountain system automatically turns on suddenly, pops up colourful musical movements here and there. When the music stops, the sprinkler is turned off for a short while and starts again leaving children and people cheering and clapping with excitement. During the weekends, 'Ho Chi minh City Street Show' as it is called is scheduled from 8 or 9 p.m. goes on whole night along the pedestrian street. These shows feature not only common street arts like magic, musical and dance performances but traditional arts and folk songs also. Vendors sell their eatables and playthings on their vending bikes.

Interestingly during the day time, however, one may neither find any stage nor water fountains. One may only find the street and

A new housing complex with high rise towers have recently been built in District Seven of Ho Chi Minh City.

local and foreign tourists walking over the stretch. In morning, people walk, jog, exercise on the stretch.

I watched from the window of my room of The Saigon Palace Hotel at Nguyen Hue street , thousands of people, most of them young, participating and watching the show. As many as six, may be more, stages were designed in the typical street style where different performances were performed simultaneously. In this charged youthful atmosphere, how can Saigon sleep!

On one side of Nguyen Hue street is situated the 68 storied high rise building Bitexco Financial Tower, built in 2010, which is the latest addition to the horizon of Ho Chi Minh City. Lotus is the national flower of Vietnam and this high rise building is designed on the shape of lotus bud having one petal opened. Other high rises like Sunwah Tower, Vietcom Bank Tower and Saigon Centre etc. are also on the same street. One of our Vietnamese friends informed us that Landmark 81 in Ho Chi Minh City is under construction and is coming up fast. Presently Landmark 72 in the city is the tallest building of the city.

About 15 metres from this stretch, work for Ho Chi Minh City Metro (underground railway) in collaboration with Japan is in

Musical performance in progress at Nguyen Hue Walking Street's 'Ho chi Minh City Street show'.

progress, and is entering its fourth year into construction of the Saigon Metro system is chugging along, The first line of Ho Chi Minh City's metro system, the Ben Thanh-Suoi Tien line, will cover 19.7km, mostly above ground, and connect the city centre with eastern districts. It is expected to begin operation in 2020, two years later than originally planned.

It deserves a special mention here that from the early days of its foundation, the city had been quite a favourite among the Indian inhabitants, since the traders from both the North and the South India had chosen it as one of the places for their settlement in Vietnam. During the early twentieth century the Indian traders had not only settled in thousands in the city but they had been able to establish their dominance in the field of small and medium trade. The Chettiyars of Tamilnadu had their monopoly in the money lending business and as such the Indian community of the traders were ill famed as money lenders. However, since it was the need of the society, people borrowed money from them under compulsion even on a very high rate of interest and in the process of repayment some had to forego their property and possession. Besides the Chettiyars the Punjabi Sikhs, the merchants or grocers from Uttar Pradesh and the Muslims had also settled in Saigon in quite a sizable number. There were around two hundred Indian families that were engaged in small business to earn their livelihood.

During the late nineteenth century four Hindu temples, a Gurdwara, and a mosque had already been built by the Indian, Hindu, Sikh and Muslim settlers in Saigon.There were four Hindu temples, a Sikh Gurdwara and a mosque built by Indian Muslims that was locally known as Indian 'Moske', in Saigon (Ho Chi Minh City). Most of the devotees visiting the Hindu temples today are Vietnamese, who visit there out of simple devotion and offer offerings. This process is continuing. The proprietary right of the temples belonged to the Hindus of the Indian origin. In course of time, however, to widen the road the deserted Gurdwara and Ganesh temple were demolished while the other three Hindu temples and the Indian moske still exist and enjoy the protection of the Government. The Hindu temples of Ho Chi Minh City present a unique confluence of two cultures.

In 1927 the Indian Society and Vietnamese intellectuals had invited the great Indian poet and Nobel laureate Rabindranath Tagore to visit Saigon. Tagore could not make it that year but he sent Dr. Kalidas Nag as his emissary with a note that on the next given opportunity he will certainly visit Saigon. Finally in 1929 when Tagore visited Saigon on a day and a half sojourn, he was accorded a grand reception and hundreds of people assembled to listen to him. Nearly half of the assembled people belonged to the Indian community.

First Indian Restaurant 'ASHOKA' at Ho Chi Minh City After the unification opened by Mr. Ashok Sharda.

On his way to Taipeh in 1945, Indian leader and freedom fighter Netaji Subhash Chandra Bose had also stayed in Saigon for several days. In 1954, Jawahar Lal Nehru, during his official visit to Vietnam, had visited Ho Chi Minh City.

In 1974, there were around 30,000 Indians belonging mostly to the Chettiyar community, migrated from Tamilnadu within a span of last two hundred years. Except a few, most of them fled away from Vietnam immediately after its liberation and unification fearing that they would be ill treated by the Communist regime, an apprehension that proved completely wrong in the following days.

Presently, according to a rough estimate there are around two thousand Indians, most of whom represent various multinational companies. One cannot conceive of a Bengali inhabitant without a Durga Puja. So today, Durga Puja is celebrated every year in Ho Chi Minh City with much fanfare. Other Indian festivals viz. Shivaratri, Pongal etc. are also celebrated in HO Chi Minh City when the Indian fraternity visits temples. On days other than the festivals hardly any Indian visits the temples and only Vietnamese

Consulate General of India organised International. Yoga Day at Ho chi Minh City. Present on the occasion were (from L ToR) Mr. Dilbagh Man Mohan Singh, President of INCHAM, Mr. Huynh Minh Thier, Chairman of HUFO, the author, a Vietnamese Yoga Teacher and Ms. Smita Pant, the Consul General of india in Ho Chi Minh City.

offer their obeisance to Hindu gods and goddesses.

Mr. Ashok Sharda, the founder of Ashoka Restaurant in Ho Chi Minh city, had established his first Indian Restaurant in Vietnam after its liberation and unification. He had migrated to Ho Chi Minh City, Vietnam from Calcutta (now Kolkata) in 1986. He was the second Indian to have settled there after 1976, the first being Mr. Shantanu Srivastava, who was earlier working in Indian Embassy and subsequently decided to resign from the Embassy and settle in Vietnam and did brisk business for few years. Presently he is back in India.

Mr. Ajay Panot, one of the founder members of Indian Chamber of Commerce (INCHAM) is permanently settled in Vietnam and is leading a happy family life with his Vietnamese wife and children. Under his presidentship INCHAM had been very active and had done lots of social work in the villages of Vietnam nearby Ho Chi Minh City.

Recently Mr. Dilbagh Man Mohan Singh has become the President and Mr. M.B. Radhakrishnan, Vice Chairman of INCHAM. Under the dynamic leadership of Mr. Dilbagh Singh, today, INCHAM team is active and has many future projects.

Today this city is one of the most developed cities of Vietnam. Ho Chi Minh City today may compete with any developed Asian City and has become an attraction for both local and foreign tourists. Parallel to the district 1, other districts have also emerged offering most modern and comfortable life along with huge high rises that have to certain extent covered the horizon during last 25 years or so. Special emphasis is laid on architecture so that it does not look like a concrete jungle alone. Ho Chi Minh City is a business centre and commercial city and its people are most co-operative and hospitable. The same is the scenario in every town and village of Vietnam.

7

CAPITAL OF RESISTANCE WAR

Thai Nguyen province situated between highland and mountains in the north of Vietnam is one among the five most developed provinces of Vietnam. In fact, committed human labour and planned development has completely changed the face of this province.

While planning about the all round development of Vietnam and that too with a greater pace, the leadership of the Communist Party of Vietnam and the administration realized that their priority should be the construction of a network of roads and highways and thereby interlinking every province, every city to even distant villages and country side, and it was due to this strategy that Vietnam could ensure all round development of each and every province. Take for instance Thai Nguyen province. Through a network of highways, express ways and roads, the province is not only linked to Hanoi, the capital city but to all the provinces, roads and highways attached to its boundary.

As a result, the Thai Nguyen province is not only a modern province in Vietnam but very shortly it is going to be linked with Ho Chi Minh City through Ho Chi Minh road.

Thai Nguyen province is also renowned for its quality tea production. Due to its favourable climatic and soil conditions and of course with the use of researches and modern technology, this province produces the best quality of tea in Vietnam. We visited

Tea Museum and Green tea gardens near the museum.

While introducing us to the historical background of the province, the Vice President of the Friendship Union informed us that after the DRV (Democratic Republic of Vietnam) came into existence, in their bid to capture Vietnam again, the French colonialists made Saigon, in the South Vietnam, a centre of their activities.

On the other hand to wage a war of resistance against the French colonialists Ho Chi Minh was in search of a place that would be inaccessible and a difficult terrain for the enemy and for this the Thai Nguyen, Tuyen Quang and Bac Can areas in the north between highland and mountains seemed to him comparatively safe.

To wage the war of resistance he needed such a place that would have been easily accessible to the freedom fighters and inaccessible to the enemy. He felt the Thai Nguyen province was the most ideal and appropriate place for the resistance war due to its inaccessible hilly and intense forest areas. At that time this province was the most backward one and was situated at a distance of about 60 kms. from Hanoi and there was hardly any means of communication.

After the end of Second World War, it was expected that France would wash its hands off Vietnam or so to say that it would grant recognition to Vietnam as an independent sovereign state, but nothing of that sort happened.

Ho Chi Minh, however, had some inkling of it and he started preparations to confront France to liberate his fatherland, but for this he needed a little more time to organize and unite the people so that with their united force the French could be successfully faced and driven out of Vietnam. So, with this end in view, he started campaign for some sort of a treaty with the French rulers and also attempted to gain more and more support of the people of France.

A resistance army was formed under the leadership of Ho Chi

President Ho Chi Minh's Memorial House in Dinh Hoa Security Zone (ATK) at Thai Nguyen Province.

Minh and Thai Nguyen province was converted into the capital of revolution and from here itself the resistance movement for complete freedom of Vietnam was started.

The French tried their level best but failed to last long before the resistance army. The total population of the area unitedly came out against the aggressors with complete dedication and commitment and added a golden chapter in the history.

On 19th December 1946, Ho Chi Minh established the Resistance War Capital in the Central Safe Zone (ATK) and conducted the nationwide war of resistance against the enemy from a small shack at the top of Khau Ty hill. While waging the war of resistance he had said on 19th December 1946 :

"We long for peace. We have to make concessions. But more we make concessions, the more the French Colonialism enriches as they are determined to rob our country one more time.

No! We would rather sacrifice all rather than losing the country, we are determined not to be slaves...Time to save the country has come. Let's sacrifice till the last drop of blood for the country. Despite hardship in resistance war, yet with determination and sacrifice, our nation will definitely come to success."

On 9th May 2005 to commemorate the glorious beginning of freedom struggle under leadership of Ho Chi Minh a 'Commemoration House' was established and in 2014 a book titled 'Uncle Ho with Thai Nguyen Photo Event' was published.

Today the same Thai Nguyen province is one of the leading provinces of Vietnam both in agriculture and industry. It is linked with Hanoi, the capital of Vietnam by a highway, through which we covered a distance of 60 kms. in just 45 minutes.

Thai Nguyen province is rich in mineral resources like iron ore, zinc etc. It has a significant place in Vietnam for its educational institutions. It also has a leading place in production of quality tea.

Author at the Tea Cultural Space, Tea Museum at Thai Nguyen Province.

Author at Green Tea Garden at Tan Cuong Hill, Thai Nguyen Province.

Thai Nguyen province is one such area that produces the best quality of green tea in Vietnam. The distinguishing feature of this province is that half of it is in the plain area while the rest half is hilly terrain. The cold weather and fertile soil of the hilly terrain is extremely suitable for the best quality of green tea that this province produces.

Green tea is quite popular among the Vietnamese for whom anytime is green tea time. They enjoy their sips of green tea in the morning, in the afternoon and after dinner. In fact, green tea has become an integral part of Vietnamese culture and so keeping this fact in mind The Tea Cultural Space Tea Museum was established and opened in 2011.

If ever you visit Thai Nguyen City, you cannot afford to miss a visit to the 25 kms. long man made Nui Coc Lake and the Tea Cultural Space Tea Museum as both of these places are situated at a distance of 5 kms. from the Tea Museum.

Tan Cuong hills are famous for the best quality green tea and while visiting various tea gardens there we finally reached the Tea Museum situated in Sai Vang village.

This Tea Museum built at an open space has since become a special tourist attraction. In 2013 an International Tea Festival was organized here where endeavours were made to establish that the green tea is the main element of history, culture and tradition of the people of Tan Cuong region. In the Tea Cultural Space Tea Museum there are three architectural sections, a reception hall an exhibition of tea planting, collecting and processing, which illustrates the history of Thai Nguyen, tea processing technique in old times and in the modern time. There is also a section that elaborates how green tea is traditionally served. Here we were served tea, the sips of which we enjoyed. The principal attraction of the Tea Museum is a 3.6 meter high ceramic Teapot. This unique teapot was designed and made by artist Nguyen Thai Son in 76 days. It is the largest ceramic teapot in Vietnam or may be in the world. Alike many other visitors, we also had a photo session with the huge kettle in the background.

After stepping out of the Tea Museum, we also paid a visit to the nearby tea gardens and were literally charmed by the beautiful landscape.

Visiting after the Tea Cultural space museum and nearby tea gardens, we proceeded towards the Nui Coc Lake. This lake has a distinguishing feature that during the war of resistance people of Thai Nguyen unitedly created a huge 25 sq. km. lake The Núi Cốc

A panoramic view of Nui Coc Lake. It is a beautiful man made lake.

A giant Buddha statue at Tam Do National Park beside Nui Coc Lake.

Lake, to provide clean water to agriculture and industry besides producing electricity to meet the demands of the province to a great extent.

Huge man made lake is approximately 25 kilometres west of the city of Thai Nguyen Province's Tam Do National Park. It is a popular visitor attraction on account of the legend associated with the 89 islands within the lake. In 2007 special feature was added by developing musical fountains. The main fountain rises to a height of over 40 metres (130 ft.) with several subsidiary fountains, which present a spectacular sight. The water fall of today Nui Coc Lake attracts a large number of Vietnamese and foreign tourists.

It is a fountain accompanied by the music played on the khen, a musical instrument of the local ethnic people.

Other attractions in the park are: a 'Fairy Tale House Underworld and Water park' with a total area of about 6 hectares (15 acres); an artificial cave system, a large fish statue; in one of the large islands of 89 islets in the lake Vietnamese traditional culture is on display with 2061 cultural and historical items, which include the Bodhisattva of Compassion with thousands of hands and eyes.

To develop the greenery all around the lake enormous number of saplings have been planted. There are several islets in the lake where tourists may enjoy the sips of tea or coffee or may even stay overnight.

The lake is located in the scenic backdrop provided by the Coc Mountain. The lake was created on the Cong River, a tributary of the Red River. The lakeshore is divided into two areas, namely the northern bank and the southern bank. The northern bank has many upscale guest houses built on slopes of the hill amidst green trees, known as keo la cham. There is a water park and also an artificial Dinosaur park on this bank.

Nui Coc Lake is the subject of a legend about 'Coc', a boy from a poor family, and 'Cong', a girl from a rich mandarin family. Despite being deeply in love with each other, Coc was not allowed to marry Cong due to the difference in their social status. Despondent, broken-hearted and pining for his lover, Coc played the flute to call Cong to his room, but she was not allowed to leave the house to meet him. Coc eventually died, whereupon fairies took pity on him and transformed him into Coc Mountain, which now surrounds the lake.

When Cong heard of her lover's fate, she began to cry, day and night. Her love was sincere and loyal, and she cried so much that it resulted in her dying and transforming into tears, which seeped to the ground and started flowing as a stream called the 'Cong River' which feeds the lake. During the summer season every year violet rose myrtle flowers bloom in the Coc mountain hill and the Nui Coc Lake. The legend is also extended to the province, which is named as Tan Cuong. Further, it is said that the famous Tan Cuong tea grown here has absorbed Cong's tears in its roots created the sweet flavor of the tea.

8

BEN TRE : KINGDOM OF COCONUT

Our journey to Ben Tre was quite a thrilling one and provided us several new informations. Within one and a half hour we reached Ben Tre, 85 kms. from Ho Chi Minh City. On our way we crossed the river Mekong through Co Chien Bridge. The inhabitation between clusters of coconut trees, flocks of clouds floating above under the blue expanse of the sky and Co-Chien River, a tributary of river Mekong flowing below had literally charmed us.

The road leading to the city had rows of coconut trees on both sides. The Hotel Ham Luong, where we were scheduled to stay was situated in a comparatively peaceful and most clean area. The hotel was named after Ham Luong river, that was flowing in front of it.

Dwarf Variety of coconut tree at Ben Tre.

Mr. Van Loe Minh, owner of 'Ca On' Vegetarian restaurant at Ben Tre, Painting of an Indian mythical character Srawan Kumar and his blind parents on the wall behind.

During our interaction with the friends of Ben Tre Friendship Union, we learnt a lot about the city Ben Tre that is known as coconuts' Kingdom for its various varieties of coconut that included Xiem Dwarf of Ben Tre. The whole province has a huge coconut growing area that produces about 562.11 million nuts per year. The average turnover from the export of coconut based products is about 160 million USD/year with more than 36 coconut products that are being exported to various countries in the world.

Presently the province is promoting and encouraging investments in manufacturing new and high added value products from coconut oil besides maintaining production and improving output from traditional products viz. desiccated coconut, coconut candy, coconut fibre, handicrafts etc.

We visited a factory named Luong Quoi Coconut Co. Ltd. at Ben Tre where we came across various coconut products that included canned coconut water, canned coconut cream, coconut edible oil, hundred per cent coconut oil and various varieties of perfumed coconut oil. The expiry date of these products varied from one year to two years.

In fact, coconut and its various products have brought progress to both the rural as well as the urban areas of the province.

While passing through the coconut producing areas we came across coconut trees that were so small in height that one could pluck coconut by raising one's hand. We were later told that it was dwarf variety that they had developed after a long research and adopting new techniques, so as to make it easier to pluck the coconuts. Although the production of coconut is still based on manual labour but the provincial administration is endeavouring to develop mechanised farming of the coconut.

Besides coconut Ben Tre is also famous for its cocoa plantation. In fact, it has a cocoa planting area of nearly half of the whole country and the quality of cocoa produced is so fine that it qualifies for export to various European countries.

Ben Tre is gradually forming specialty fruit tree cultivation area with high yielding varieties in some of its districts focusing on building specialised areas for provincial key fruits like green skin pomelo, durian, mangosteen, rambutan etc. and combining ecotourism with intercropping fish-fruit trees.

While observing the progress and development of Ben Tre, we were amazed to see that a province that had been totally ruined during the war of liberation; a province that once had no infrastructure since all the government offices, clinics and schools besides the coconut farms were all destroyed; a province where there was no bridge and one had to cross the river Mekong through ferry or boat; the same province has turned into one among the most progressing provinces of Vietnam.

Multistoried buildings, wide roads, highways and bridges besides establishment of various industries are all pointing towards a hard earned progress of Ben Tre.

While returning for Kolkata from Ho Chi Minh City we were waiting after check in at the Ho Chi Minh City Airport. We bought sandwiches and coffee. While munching sandwiches we were reminded of Ben Tre and its coconut trees as our sandwiches had coconut in it.

9

LAO CAI : FAST UPCOMING CITY BORDERING CHINA

My visit to Lao Cai had been a thrilling and enriching one. In fact, it was a dream come true for me to observe how 25 ethnic minorities out of 54 ethnic groups in Vietnam, lived in harmony in this Northwest mountainous region of Lao Cai.

Author at Lao Cai International Border Gate.

Lao Cai has its vital locational and strategic importance too as this border town is adjacent to Yunnan province of China. It is a frontier and high mountainous province. The word Lao Cai means

'Old Town' in English. In the modern times this city was officially established in 1907 and this is the city situated in an area through which China had invaded Vietnam to teach it a lesson in 1979. As compared to various areas of Vietnam, till 1990 this area was quite a backward one and since 1991 special care was taken to ensure its all round development.

It takes about four hours to reach Lao Cai city from Hanoi through six lanes' Lao Cai Express Way. Lao Cai city is about 345 kms. from the Metropolis Hanoi by road route and about 296 kms. by rail route. Throughout the journey we noticed massive afforestation and plantation on both the sides of the expressway as also on the hills. All through the hilly terrain we found thousands and thousands of trees that were planted during last five to six years for aforestation. We could hardly find any barren patch. It was greenery all around and special care was taken to make sure that the trees should stand erect and are not slipshod. Miles after miles the saplings of trees were supported by bamboo sticks.

Maize and rice were cultivated in the plain area besides various types of herbs. We were so engrossed in the lovely landscape and greenery of the area that despite time consumed, we felt that our journey had ended rather too soon. We also realized that for meagre immediate gain, the man mindlessly chops off the trees and ruins the environment but the same man, if he so wishes, could devise ways to utilize the wealth of the nature and may even increase its natural beauty manifold as we witnessed in Lao Cai.

This wide scale afforestation and greenery in Vietnam is not being achieved without hindrance. Whenever the administration has been slack or the awareness of the people has decreased, for some monetary gains the people have indulged in excesses against the nature. So such achievements in the field of environment require constant vigil. There had been a time when a lot of timber was exported from Vietnam. Today, however, there is a complete ban on export of timber from Vietnam.

Without any more deviation let us now come back to our visit to Lao Cai. As soon as we entered the city, at a little distance from the road we found the construction work of hundreds of buildings in full swing and in a stage of near completion. All the crossings and intersections were aesthetically well decorated. In fact, it implies to all small and big towns of Vietnam. Wherever you go, you would find new construction work in full swing and cranes all around.

The present day Lao Cai may be termed as a modern city of Vietnam having big malls, wide roads, wide footpaths for pedestrians, multistoreyed buildings and high rises, schools, colleges, hospitals, and all the amenities required for a modern living. There are dozens of various star hotels. According to the Government statistics nearly 1.2 million tourists visited Lao Cai in 2013. Naturally, the number of tourists must have increased in the succeeding years.

While passing through the city we halted and enjoyed tea, coffee and snacks at various places and then travelled around 10 kms. from the centre of the city to see the Vietnam border with China. In fact, we were extremely eager to see it. We got an opportunity to visit Vietnam-China border situated in the middle of the Red river.

On the other side of the border the Chinese City He Kou was situated demonstrating its magnificence. We were so close to the Chinese border that the people on the other side could hear us had we shouted. On the right side at a distance of about fifty to sixty metres there had been the Nam Thi River of Vietnam that meets the Red River of China. It was a wonderful confluence between the two rivers. How wonderful it would have been had there also been a confluence of the hearts of the two peoples.

We found trading activities in full swing between Lao Cai and He Kou cities. Hundreds of small traders from both the cities were standing in a row along with their wares, ferrying their goods from this side to that, but yes, for this they have to obtain permission from their respective governments, and this coming and going continues comfortably throughout the day.

High-rise buildings of both Lao Cai and He Kou towns were in sight and one could see the magnificent four storied building of China Duty Free Shop on the other side of the border to lure the Vietnamese consumers. We could locate through binoculars several Vietnamese nationals visiting the said building. In response Vietnam has also opened a lavish high mall in its territory wherein a huge quantity of various consumer goods 'Made in Vietnam' are on display for sales. There are about 20 to 30 per cent Chinese products as well besides few shops rented by the Chinese.

Although Lao Cai province is famous for its agricultural production but it also has some industrial units, the number of which are on constant rise. Foreign units are also being invited here for investment, to establish their industries to earn profit and to help in the development of Vietnam. Mineral resources, water and forest wealth is in abundance in this area. There exist lots of possibilities for fertilizer and chemical industry.

There is hundred per cent literacy in Lao Cai province. Every child completes his primary education and minimum basic health service is provided to each and every citizen. It is difficult to make out through dress who is rich and who is poor. Everybody has an own house or a flat, howsoever small it may be. Is it necessary to write here that everybody has a motorbike?

The total population of Lao Cai province is about 1.2 million, that includes the population of the hill and the plains areas. Most of the ethnic groups live in distant hilly areas and are comparatively a bit backward than those living in the plains. These groups are steadily on the path of progress due to the planned governmental endeavours and awareness among the people. The government is undertaking all the endeavours on various fronts to lift them from their backwardness and to include them in the mainstream society.

Lao Cai is an eco-friendly and quiet city by all standards. It is so quiet that after late evenings it may be called a sleepy city.

It seems that in Vietnam every city or town, big or small, is being converted into a tourist centre to attract more and more tourists and Lao Cai also is one such city that welcomes the tourists. Obviously, therefore, the people of the city are cordial, co-operative, warm, kind hearted and above all emotional to certain extent.

I was amazed to see the all round development of the city and yes, I enjoyed each and every moment of my stay there.

After my visit to this city, I arrived at the conclusion that the Vietnamese officials are committed to beat the magnificence of the Chinese City and having seen their determination, I am sure, they will succeed.

10

HA LONG BAY : WORLD NATURAL HERITAGE SITE

Ha Long bay located in the northeast of Vietnam, about 170 kms. east of Hanoi is famous for its scenic ocean Karst topography and is included in the lists of natural wonders of the world. It has an area of 1,553 sq. km. in the Gulf of Tonkin and includes about 1,600 islands and islets forming a spectacular seascape of limestone pillars. Ha Long Bay is internationally famous, twice recognized as a World Natural Heritage Site by UNESCO for the majestic beauty

'Kissing Rocks' at Ha Long Bay.

of its dense rocks, islands and natural caves.

Ha Long Bay was formed by millions of years of geological changes, which created thousands of islands. Hidden inside there are beautiful caverns such as Sung Sot, Thien Cung, Trinh Nu, Thien Canh Son caves and Thien Cung Grotto.

The outstanding features of Ha Long Bay include the magnificent towering limestone pillars and associated notches, arches and caves, that are exceptionally well developed and among the best of its type in the world.

The exceptional beauty and charm of Ha Long Bay has made it an outstanding tourist destination.

There is an outstanding local legend about this bay according to which ever since the first settlement of the country, Vietnam had to face attacks from the sea route. Knowing this, the Jade Emperor sent Mother Dragon and her child to help the Vietnamese against the invaders. When the enemy ships were approaching, the dragons flew downward from the sky and spat countless pearls into the sea, which turned into myriad of jade islands. They got linked together to create a solid wall that blocked the approach of the enemy ships, which crashed into the rocks and were torn to pieces. After driving away the invaders, the Mother Dragon and her child were so charmed by the beauty of the bay that they decided to stay there itself rather than returning to heaven. Where the Mother Dragon landed was called Ha Long, which means 'Bay of Descending Dragons'. Her child settled in Bai Tu Long Bay and where their tails entwined is Bach Long Vi island.

When I had first visited this area in the nineties, it was an underdeveloped area and the development work had just been started in the hollow mountains by country boats.

Again in the year 2015, when I visited this spot, I was amazed to find it converted into a world class tourist centre with hundreds of hotels of various categories in the mountains providing all sorts of facilities and comfort to the tourists. Two storeyed motorboats with dining hall, washroom, souvenir vendors and other facilities had replaced the old country boats and carried tourists to the hollowed mountains, that are beautified and decorated manually without disturbing the ecology and environment.

About three kilometres from Ha Long Bay centre, a non-resident Vietnamese has developed an island during the first decade of twenty first century that attracts thousands of tourists for its amazing amusement and recreational activities that include 'Dolphin Dance' in an indoor pool. In an open area of this newly developed island there are numerous fountains that create human figures in water and depict various folk-tales along with musical presentation. There are a number of recreational activities in the island where from a child to an old man finds enjoyment and entertainment.

For overnight stay there are a few guest houses, eateries of various varieties, souvenir shops. The whole area is surrounded by thick forest.

Visit to this island is a costly affair as for every amusement one has to pay handsomely.

11

A BEAUTIFUL HILL STATION : SA PA

Visiting Sa Pa was as though we were visiting Nainital Hill Station in India where Naini Lake, a natural freshwater-body surrounded by panoramic seven hills of Shivalik range of the Himalya, is situated amidst the township of Nainital in Uttarakhand State in North of India. Founded by the British in 1841 and its altitude is about 1943m above sea level, Nainital is now a popular hill station of India.

Scenic beauty of hill station Sa Pa

Likewise the history of Sa Pa Hill station also has its roots in French colonial period. At 1650 m above sea level, it is situated in Vietnam's remote northwest Hoang Lien Son mountain range near Chinese border. Sa Pa and its surrounding region hosts many hilly tribes besides providing rice terraces, lush vegetation and Phan Si Pang (Fansipan), highest peak in Indochina. It is most popular picturesque resort of Vietnam.

Before 1901 Sa Pa city, the famous Hill Station of Vietnam had been a cluster of several villages inhabited by various tribal ethnic groups and was nearly cut off from the mainland.

In 1901 a French administrator and wanderer visited this area and was literally charmed by the beauty of its landscape. In fact, this cold area of Sa Pa was a great relief from the scorching and sweltering heat of the plains of Vietnam for the high ranking French officials. A military garrison Cha Pa was established by the French here to keep a watch over North Vietnam as a whole. By 1906 a railway track had already been laid between Hanoi and Lao Cai and Sa Pa was linked by road to Lao Cai and slowly due to its cold weather and pleasant landscape it became famous as 'Tonkinese Alps'. In 1922 it earned the distinction of being the 'Summer residence' of the Governor General of Indochina.

In due course of time, however, Sa Pa became a hill station and 'Summer Capital' of the French colonialists and as a result nightly sleeper coach travels started from Hanoi and several hotels were established to provide shelters to the visitors.

In 1947 the Viet Minh Liberation Troop launched a massive attack and the French had to suffer a severe reverse. However, they recovered from the set back soon and by sending additional force recaptured the area.

By that time this North-Western area had turned into a war field and the grip of the French over Sa Pa had loosened. Forced by an attitude of vengeance the French indulged into indiscriminate bombing of Sa Pa and as a result most of the French Villas, government office buildings and sanatoriums were completely destroyed. Even the church property suffered a great loss.

After the liberation, Sa Pa was no more a summer Capital but became famous as a hill station and since then this small city continued to be the centre of attraction for foreign tourists as well as for the tourists of the country.

We set off for Sa Pa from Lao Cai by road. We enjoyed our ride through spiralling roads and pleasant landscapes. One of the officials of Lao Cai Friendship Union invited us to have tea at his residence on way and we could not refuse. We had to visit his residence, that was spread over several acres (one acre is equal to 4840 square yards or 0.405 hectare). The very building appeared

Sa Pa Church, which is also known as Stone Church or the Holy Rosary Church.

People of Various ethnic minorities in front of Sa Pa Church engaged in their traditional activites.

like a palacial one having a small pond in the campus. An old man was cleaning the pond of the fallen tree leaves, and at a distance a woman was also cleaning the area of the fallen tree leaves. Later we learnt that the septuagenarian old man was the owner of the house, who had earned money through trade and had built this palacial building with a big garden in it. He had to labour hard for nearly four to five hours every day for the upkeep of the garden. In fact, every Vietnamese labours hard and this gentleman was no exception to it. The garden was really beautiful and well maintained. There were several fruit laden trees besides plants of numerous herbs and about a hundred types of rare flowers, the saplings of which he had imported from various countries. All the family members manually worked for the upkeep of the house and had also hired a helper to help them.

Having enjoyed our tea and fresh plucked plums from the orchard we set off for Sa Pa and within ten minutes we were there. There was a big lake in the middle of the city having trees and greenery all around. There were wide footpaths by the side of the lake and benches for the visitors to sit and relax. There were quite wide roads alongside and there were rows of hotels and buildings. The hotels belonged to various categories and their charges varied from 10 to

100 USD per night to suit various categories of the tourists. There was no encroachment anywhere and the whole city was most clean. Although the new cable car and the host of large hotels being built with apparent disregard for the mountain environment have perhaps reduced the charm of Sa Pa to a certain extent, yet a short walk or drive still provide a pleasant view.

In 1935, right in the centre of Sa Pa town near the lake , a Catholic Church was built by French which was restored three times. It was first restored in 1995 and then again restored twice in 2007. It is known as Stone Church or The Holy Rosary Church. The Church has a big compound which usually is crowded by local people as well as tourists. The local people most of whom are of tribal minorities groups relax, some sell various items to the tourists. Throngs of venders can be found in the streets aggressively selling their wares. It has become more like a market place.

Author interacting with Mr. Pham Vanitac, at his garden house on the outskirt of Sa Pa.

We found several families enjoying the light cool evening in the campus of a church. Since it was a lean period for the tourists, most of the visitors belonged to various ethnic groups of Vietnam. There was an open stadium typed stage where various cultural performances take place every day.

People were quite friendly and sociable and warmly greeted us saying 'An Do', which meant 'Indian'. Some captured us in the frames of their selfies. We were pleasantly surprised to find an Indian restaurant in such a distant place, that was being run by an Indian family.

12

A REMOTE MOUNTAINOUS VILLAGE : TA PHIN

The population of Vietnam consists of 54 ethnic groups and 85 per cent of the population belongs to Kinh ethnic group. There is another ethnic group named Cham that has a population of about 150,000 who believe they were Hindus and their ancestors had come from India. Presently about 100,000 of them are Hindus

Author with a wonan belonging to 'H' mong ethnic group at Ta Phin.

A Village woman preparing tea at Ta Phin village.

and about 50,000 are Muslims. Among the 54 ethnic groups in Vietnam there are also certain tribes that live in the distant hilly areas of Vietnam.

One such hilly area or rather a famous hill station of Vietnam is Sa Pa situated on the distant North West of Vietnam and about 12 kms. from Sa Pa along National Road AD to Lao Cai there is a small hamlet named Ta Phin. In recent years it has become a tourist attraction for its Ta Phin cave that comprises several separate caverns and features various stalactite formations; Silver Waterfall that offers an excellent view of waterfall and the mountains beyond; besides Mountain Fansipan that may be reached only on foot from Sa Pa. This time we had the opportunity to visit this beautiful hamlet. The total road leading to it was cemented that had fragments here and there. In fact, all the villages and hamlets situated on difficult hilly terrains in Vietnam are all linked by cemented roads. Using the serpentine road and travelling for about two hours to cover a distance that should have taken only half an hour as the driver of our car being unacquainted of the road strayed very often and this proved a boon to us as we strayed into various villages, which we would have otherwise skipped. We enjoyed our journey and felt as if we were passing through the hilly areas of Meghalaya, Manipur or Arunachal situated in the North East of India.

Finally, though late, we reached Ta Phin Village that had about 100 houses and a population of about 700-800. Most of the houses were made of bricks having tin roofs, besides some wooden hutments. The tallest among the houses was a two storeyed one. The village had covered drainage system. Every house had water and electricity connections. Although most of the houses had Liquefied Petroleum Gas ovens, still some of the houses used fire wood to save money. Almost every household had cell phone, motorbike and television set. The facial appearances, dresses, type of food were slightly different from the mainstream Vietnamese society. Of late, however, some people have started to dress like the common Vietnamese.

Our host Mr. Dat (full name: Giang A Dat) belongs to 'H' mong ethnic group, and gives a portion of his house to visiting foreign tourists on rent. His this 'home-stay' is named 'Heaven Ly'. Dat has married a girl Vu Thi Ly belonging to 'Tay' ethnic group. During our conversation Dat confessed that he had been charmed by the beauty of Ly while he was working in Sa Pa and that they both were sharing loving relationship and understanding after marriage. They had two children - a boy and a girl - and were expecting a third one.

Dat offered us food and after having it we had a long chat for about an hour and a half. He told us that till ten years back they were quite backward and to certain extent lazy too. It was common among the villagers to have eight to ten children and avoid being educated. They were satisfied with one crop a year using stored seeds that were quite inferior in quality. Obviously, the yield was quite less in quantity and inferior in quality. Yet, they somehow managed with the same. There were, and still are, united families, three generations living under the same roof with each other. In fact, the tradition of United Family system in Vietnamese society still persists.

Today, however, quite a lot has changed. Every village or hamlet has a primary school, and a health centre. Every household has a water tap and electricity. Villages have covered drainage system and every house has a toilet. However, old habits die hard and so there are countable few people, who still prefer to defecate in the open forest due to their traditional habit. The Government of

Vietnam provides stainless steel water tanks to store water on the roof top, yet there are some people, who utilize it to store their food grains. There is no child, who does not go to school.

Dat told us that the awareness among the people has so increased that the families now prefer to have four children on an average. If the present awareness persists, may be in the days to come a family would have one or two children on an average. Dat confided that even he intended to have four children.

Presently, the Government provides quality seeds and subsidized fertilizer to every family, as a result of which not only the yield has increased but the people are now growing two crops a year. Now, the people have sufficient food grains and are self reliant, so far as the food grains are concerned. There may still be poverty but nobody has to die out of hunger or malnutrition.

In the morning we visited several houses in the village and interacted with the families with the help of our Vietnamese friend Minh. During conversation village elder informed us through our interpreter Minh that every child, went to school and completed his primary education at least. Those willing to continue their studies go to secondary schools and for Higher Secondary studies one has to go to Sa Pa.

He further informed us that there were crèches cum kindergartens where working women could leave their children while going to work and could collect them when they are back from work. It was surprising and to some extent unbelievable for us that at such a distant place they had arrangements for crèches and kindergartens. When the old man found traces of surprise over our face, he insisted in our going with him to see for ourselves.

To erase out our apprehensions we visited the nearby school and witnessed a small but beautiful crèche cum kindergarten house on the walls of which there were several beautiful pictures painted to allure the children. We realized, the village elder was right.

There were two principal reasons for the children of such a distant place to go to school for studies. The first being that the cultivation had become comparatively less laborious. The Government provided better seeds, fertilizer and technical equipments for easy cultivation and as a result the dependence over children for agriculture had decreased. Secondly, by organizing various educational camps from time to time in various districts on behalf of the government the villagers are led to realize the importance of education in life and obviously, therefore, they are drawn towards higher studies.

During our interaction we also came to know a very important fact that the people of all the ethnic groups of Vietnam had taken part in the Liberation War of Vietnam, and it was none other than Ho Chi Minh, who personally went among them to inspire them to actively participate in the Liberation War and directed his party cadres to prepare them for the revolution.

During the revolutionary movement (1943 - 45 and 1946 - 54) throughout the North-West, the ethnic groups staunchly supported the Liberation War. Party Cells and the Guerilla Bases were virtually established in every remote district. The Indochina Communist Party appealed directly to the ethnic minorities for their participation in the movement.

We were, in fact, overwhelmed by our twenty hours' sojourn in this small village of distant North West of Vietnam, not because we had visited a village with mountainous landscape of Vietnam but because of the warmth and intimacy with which the local inhabitants met and greeted us as a friendly Indian. Some treated us with local delicacies while some other invited us over tea and dinner. An elderly woman greeted us with words 'Ando' (Indian) and forcibly gave us few fruits to eat on our way back. Needless to say that such small incidents leave an everlasting impression that one cherishes all through one's life.

So, it was quite reassuring for us to see for ourselves that the change was coming, though its pace was slow in the mountainous areas.

13

CHAM ROOTS IN INDIA

It was 2010, a millennium year of Thang Long-Hanoi, the capital of Vietnam when many celebrations and events were being organised to mark the one thousand years of the ancient city. An International Conference for Vietnamese Literature was one of those many events organized in Hanoi at the initiative of poet Huu Thinh, the chairman of Vietnam Writers' Association. I and four of my colleagues were in Hanoi to participate in the said conference where very many eminent poets of Vietnamese as well as other ethnic groups were participating. It was there, that I met Inrasara, the scholar and poet of the Cham language. He was full of enthusiasm and energy. In my very first meeting I was connected

Cham scholar Inrasara, his wife inrahani and their sons.

Inscription written in Sanskrit (8 Lines) and in old Khmer (25 Lines), dated 639 of thsi era. The text relates several donations to God Shiva.

to him with a cord of friendship. During the conference, we had many sittings in which we interacted on various aspects of Cham language, literature, culture and traditions in length.

Actually, the Cham ethnic group is one of the fifty four ethnic minority groups of Vietnam whose ancestors had established a Hindu Kingdom founded by Sri Mara in Central Vietnam The Hindu Kingdom had lasted for around fourteen hundred years. The Cham people have absorbed Hinduism, Buddhism and Islam and are strongly influenced by the Indian civilization and culture. They have integrated and reconciled the three religions in their own way, resulting in the creation of their unique religious tradition.

Around second century B.C. a convoy of few Indian maritime traders had set off for Swarnadweep (Vietnam, Cambodia, Laos) from Champa Nagari (Bhagalpur, Bihar). By the time it reached the ports of Bengal and Odisha few more convoys joined it. After months of marine journey the convoy finally dropped anchor at Tien Sa port at Da Nang and at the Cham Island in Hoi An near Da Nang. This very fact, therefore, proves that the relations between Da Nang and India are as old as second century B.C. Initially for 100 to 150 years, thereafter, both India and Vietnam were engaged in brisk trade with each other but subsequently in due course of time the Indian traders were so fascinated by the beauty of the landscapes and that of the women folk of Central Vietnam that they opted to settle there and with this end in view they took along themselves some people from the royal lineage or those with martial prowess for their safety and security, some Brahmins to perform their religious rituals and some low caste people to serve them. In due course of time with the common consensus of the natives, who were highly influenced by the colourful culture of the Hindus, a Hindu Kingdom was established in Vietnam. Amaravati was the first Hindu Kingdom in Vietnam with Simhapura as its Capital and Da Nang was a part and parcel of it. Subsequently, four more Hindu Kingdoms were established in the Central part of Vietnam. Since the Hindus had migrated to Vietnam or rather Da Nang from Champa Nagari (Bhagalpur, Bihar) they were termed as Champas or the Chams and the Kingdom they established as Champa (Hindu) Kingdom, that having been established during second century A.D. remained in existence till the fifteenth century when those were invaded and defeated by Le Thanh Tong, the king of the Dai Viet Kingdom in 1471.

The term 'Champa' has its origin in Pauranic mythological literature in Sanskrit, Pali wherein it is mentioned as Champa, Champapuri, Champa Nagari etc. According to the Pauranic literature Champa was the name of the son of Pritulaksha, a descendent of Anu, who had founded the city of Champapuri. Champa was also the capital of Emperor Bimbisara (544-493 B.C.) who established his Magadh empire from Champa (Bhagalpur) to Varanasi at the bank of river Ganga. The word Cham or Champa has been derived from Champapuri or Champa Nagari.

The culture of Vietnam in totality, inclusive of religion, has extensive influence of India, is conspicuous and the culture of the Cham ethnic group, has startling similarities with the Indian Culture to a great extent, one may perceive, Cham community to be a part of an Indian Community. Of course, with great adeptness, the Champa people have Vietnamised quite a lot of Indianness in their culture and have successfully endeavoured to change themselves with the time. Close observations and informations of their culture lead us to believe that the similarity of the culture with the Indian one is inherent in nature rather being adopted or imported from India.

The Cham had introduced Indian technique of rice cultivation during 4th and 5th century or may be even earlier, which they had carried with them from India. Well-known historian Nguyen Khac Vien agrees to this basic fact in his book 'Vietnam : A long History' although he goes on to add that Cham belong to one of the Malayo Polynesian group. He writes –" The Cham already knew how to obtain two rice crops a year and that a system of hydraulic works, the remains of which suggest greater sophistication that those built by the Vietnamese at that time."

Dance plays an important and integral part in the spiritual and cultural life of Chams most of which have its origin in India. Traditional musical instruments e.g. Giang (Mridang), Banung (drum), Ceng (gong), Xarani (horn, similar to the Indian Shahnai), Grong (tinttinnabulum) provide the dance rhythm. Giang or the Mridang is the most important instrument for its strong and forceful sounds during the dance performances in popular or Royal forms. Today, these dances are performed not only on the festive occasions but on Cham heritage sites also for the tourist. I have witnessed these dances a number of times in My Son, Hoi An and in theatre Halls in Da Nang.

Front view of cham (Hindu) Tample Tower at Po Nagar, Nha Trang.

Handicrafts of Champa community particularly in textile, those of handlooms, terracotta, gold and silver pots and jewellery and sculptures are strikingly similar to Indian ones. In 2nd century B.C. to 5th century, a large number of Indians settled in the central Vietnam. They not only carried with them artifacts like jewellery and pottery but some craftsmen also, who under the patronage of Champa Kings locally manufactured hundreds of thousands of such pieces in their native Indian forms and style and at times mixed it with local style. This impact and influence of Indian craftsmanship that enriched the Vietnamese art and culture may be witnessed in various artifacts that are displayed in various museums in Vietnam.

The most wonderful and amazing similarity I came across is in language. According to the facts available, the mother tongue of the Chams belonged to the family of Sanskrit. In fact in the ancient times it was Sanskrit itself. Subsequently, however, in course of time it underwent a change in script and dialect. It may not be coincidence that the vowels and consonants used in the Cham language even today are almost identical to those of Sanskrit/ Hindi, so much so that even their pronunciations are almost identical. In the early days of the foundation of the Champa Kingdom, the content of the iscriptions was mainly in Sanskrit. By the 4th Century, the content of the inscriptions was a mixture of Sanskrit and Cham which seems to be formed, in course of time, with the influence of Pali, Odiya or South Indian language scripts.

It is, however, significant to mention here that the Hindus or the chams or the champas were never treated by the native Vietnamese as aggressors or foreigners nor were they driven out of the Vietnamese soil after the decline of their kingdoms. On the contrary they were assimilated in the main stream of the Vietnamese society. Unlike the Hindus of Indian origin the Chinese in the northern parts of Vietnam were treated with disdain and contempt after their defeat at the hands of the native Vietnamese in the tenth century and were evicted from the Vietnamese soil. This distinction in treatment with the Hindus or the Chams of Indian origin is the beauty of mutual relations between India and Vietnam which is unparalleled in the history.

Today for all practical purposes one does not find the existence of the Cham (Hindu) ethnic group in Da Nang. Their population all over Vietnam is 161,729 according to 2009 census. They are mostly settled in Quang Nam Binh Dinh, Phu Yen, Ninh Thua, Binh Thuan, Tay Ninh and An Giang provinces, but the ruins of numerous Hindu temples, that are locally known as Cham Temple Towers and which were built between seventh and fourteenth century still stand mute but glaring witness to the past cultural links between India and Vietnam and keep on reminding the presence of the erstwhile Hindu kingdom.

I will quote Mr. Than Phan, a Cham liberal muslim and a scholar whom I met in 2017 during the conference in Da Nang organized by Embassy of India in Vietnam, DAFO, VIFA of Da Nang City _"In addition to their (Cham) religious beliefs, tangible cultural heritage, such as scripts, temples and sculptures, all have their cultural origins in India, and are still used by the Cham to serve the rites, festivities, and daily life. Today, these tangible and intangible heritage have become an indispensable part of the cultural, social, and religious life of Cham people."

14

CITY OF HINDU TEMPLES : MY SON

My Son was declared as a 'World Heritage Site' by UNESCO on 1st December, 1999 and is possibly the longest inhabited archeological site, much of which was destroyed by the carpet bombing by the US aggressors during war. In fact, My Son is a Hindu temple complex built by the Champa, who ruled South and Central Vietnam from 3rd century until 1832. Upon their succession, the Champa Kings, built temple complexes at My Son.

The Champa people or the Chams were predominantly Hindus and the temples at My Son are mostly dedicated to the Hindu deity

City of Hindu Temples.

City of Hindu Temple.

Shiva. The earliest temples were built of wood in the 4th century. Those structures were later destroyed by a massive fire, the exact cause of which is still unknown. Subsequent kings rebuilt those temples first in wood, then close fitted bricks with no mortar and finally in lime stone. Most of the surviving structures of the temples in My Son are of bricks.

During my first sojourn in Da Nang in 1982, I could not visit My Son, which was earlier known as Simhapura, the capital of Amaravati, the first Hindu Kingdom in Vietnam, as the road was not at all motorable due to the excessive bombing by the US. The aggressors had not spared even My Son, the temple town of the Hindu Kingdom, founded by King Bhadraverman. In most of the survived temples in My Son Lord Shiva was the presiding deity. Idols of various other deities viz. Shiva Linga – Yoni, Brahma, Vishnu, Parvati and others were also installed in the temple complexes.

After the decline and defeat of the Hindu Kingdoms in the 15th Century at the hands of Da Viet dynasty, all the temples not only in My Son but in other parts of Vietnam also, were not destroyed or damaged. In due course of time, however, the My Son temple complexes were largely forgotten and were reclaimed by the jungle. The city was inaccessible since it was surrounded by hills on three sides and river Thu Von on the fourth. It got lost in the oblivion.

In 1898, however, the Frenchman M.C. Paris rediscovered the complex during the French occupation of Vietnam. Subsequently, two French scholoars L. Finot and H. Parmentier conducted extensive research in the area and documented in detail about its past.

In 1975 My Son was known only to a handful of historians, intellectuals and of course a few archaeologists. After the liberation and unification of Vietnam, the government paid its attention towards it and in 1980, finally a team of Polish experts and archaeologists were invited and the restoration work started in joint collaboration. Subsequently, with the assistance of the government, the specialists from Italy, Japan and Germany also undertook the challenging task, and by January 2009 restored some of the temple sites.

It is, however, an irony that the Indian archaeologists remained indifferent towards it and no initiative came from their side to

Dancing Shiva Tympanum of 8th century exhibited at My Son ci.

Performance of Apsara dance for tourists at My son with Cham Temple Towers in Background.

extend a helping hand in the restoration work. After repeated persuasion by the Indo-Vietnam Solidarity Committee, finally, the Ministry of External Affairs, Government of India, requested the Archaeological Survey of India to restore the temple sites at My Son. It took about four years to arrive at decision and finally in 2016 a team of experts proceeded towards My Son for restoration of some temple tower sites.

While writing my book titled "Traces of Indian Culture in Vietnam" I had visited My Son along with my colleague Kusum Jain and my guide Phuong, eminent historian and specialist on Cham culture, in 2009. By that time My Son had already developed as one of the most attractive tourist centres in Vietnam, with utmost modern tourist facilities. The Government of Vietnam had in the meanwhile, built a museum wherein around hundred Cham artifacts, steles and rock inscriptions are on display.

We also visited the Cham temple tower sites where the restoration work was going on in full swing. In one of the temples we found six to seven defused bomb-shells stored in an enclosure along with Shivlinga idol. Those bomb shells were the mute witnesses of the excesses carried on by the US, even not sparing the ancient sites that were the cultural heritage of mankind.

Subsequently, I was taken to a cultural show where a Vietnamese dancer performed an 'Apsara Dance' that depicted the various 'mudras' (postures) that are sculpted in the various temple towers replicating Indian sculptures.

During my next visit to My Son, I was amazed to observe some remarkable changes in the city and the areas around. Last time we had to tread the area on foot while this time we were provided a battery operated car. Dozens of souvenir shops had come up in the area with attractive terracotta idols of various Hindu deities besides Apsara and local handicraft items of Vietnam. A few eateries to cater to the visitors have also come up. Many guest houses with updated amenities at reasonable cost have also come up while earlier there was a dearth of it. The whole area was beautifully made over to fascinate the visitors from all over the world besides the local ones.

It is also an irony that at a place that represented the Indian Culture, the presence of Indian visitors was most minimal.

The Government of Vietnam has preserved these heritage sites not for any religious consideration but to project the ancient culture of the Cham (Hindu) Kingdoms.

The only thing that puzzles me is that why the original name of the capital 'Simhapura' was rechristened as 'My Son'.

However, My Son is one of the strongest bonds between India and Vietnam that reminds that India and Vietnam had a long cultural link that dated back to the first century or may be even earlier.

15

MUSEUM OF CHAM SCULPTURES

In Da Nang there is another bridge that connects India and Vietnam and this magnificent bridge is the Da Nang Museum of Cham Sculptures.

For the first time when I was about to enter the main gate of the museum, I had a strange feeling as if I was entering an Indian museum. The ambience and the artifacts on display were so identical that it was almost difficult to distinguish it from the Indian ones. Obviously, it presents a strong evidence of around 2000 years' old or may be even more, cultural link between India and Vietnam.

Da Nang Museum of Cham Sculptures, Da Nang.

Naturally, it was quite thrilling for me to witness closeness between Indian and Vietnamese culture and I only wished the people of India to personally see for themselves the artifacts, rock inscriptions in Sanskrit, numerous idols of myriad Hindu deities excavated and recovered from various sites in Central Vietnam and housed in this museum. Presently there are about 2000 objects in the Cham Museum, of which about 288 are neatly categorized and artistically displayed inside the museum while 187 are displayed in the garden outside and about 1200 are kept in the store room. Visitors are taken on a round of the Museum by trained and well informed guides, who bring alive to them the rich and glorious past of their country.

Why only the Da Nang Museum of Cham Sculptures, the souvenir stalls in the campus of the museum that sell terracotta idols, purses, hand bags, scarves, metallic jewellery etc. as souvenirs to the visitors and tourists; their wares are also quite identical to Indian handicrafts. I wished the people of India had visited the old and golden chapters of history of the cultural link between India and Vietnam.

Around 2000 artifacts, were recovered through excavations at various sites of Da Nang and its nearing areas and which include numerous 7th to 14th century idols of myriad Hindu deities viz. Rama, Sita, Shiva, Vishnu, Brahma, Krishna, Saraswati, MahishaMardini, Indra, Ganesha etc. This museum representing age-old Indian culture has the largest display outside India.

A visit to the Champa Museum in Da Nang takes the visitor back to about eight centuries when a vibrant Hindu culture had nourished in the remote coastal villages of Central Vietnam; when it celebrated its prosperity and dominance through the worship of huge sculptures of various deities housed in the sanctum sanctorum and the outer precincts of the temple-towers standing majestically over the landscape bringing alive the rich religious and social heritage of the earlier Hindu or the Cham or the Champa civilization.

Situated on the banks of the river Han, that flows majestically through the city, the Champa Museum in Da Nang, overlooked by mountains in the background, is one of the several small museums at the various temple-tower sites like My Son, Chien Dan (Chandan) etc. There is a separate division dedicated to the Cham sculptures inside the main history museums in Ho Chi Minh City and Hanoi.

The museum at Da Nang is unique in that it houses the largest number of artifacts and relics of the Champa civilization dating from the 7th century.

It was built in 1915 by the Ecole Francoised' Extreme-Orient (EFEO) to exhibit the collection of artifacts gathered through the excavations of various sites from the Quang Binh to the Binh Dinh provinces in Central Vietnam.

The most impressive building of the Champa Museum in Da Nang was designed by two French architects Delaval and Auclair, who incorporated the architectural styles of the Champa temple-towers, thereby lending it style and grace. Spread over two huge floors this large and spacious museum displays about 300 sandstone and terracotta artifacts. The outer environs of the building are beautifully landscaped with neatly trimmed hedges and the trees are planted to provide shade to the visitors. The artifacts are displayed so strategically at the entrance and flanking the staircases that it provides a glimpse of the rich collection inside the museum.

Presently there are about 2000 objects in the Cham Museum, of which about 288 are neatly categorized and artistically displayed inside the museum while 187 are displayed in the garden outside and about 1200 are kept in the storeroom. Visitors are taken on a round of the Museum by trained and well informed guides, who bring alive to them the rich and glorious past of their country.

The bronze, sandstone and terracotta artifacts are most neatly

Ganesha, 7th Century at Da Nang Museum of Cham Scnlptures, Da Nang.

arranged according to the provinces where those were found and are displayed accordingly in different pavilions viz. Tra Kieu pavilion, the Quang Nam corridor, the Quang Tri pavilion, the My Son pavilion, the Qung Nai pavilion and the Binh Dinh pavilion. A huge wall map on display marks the extent and the boundaries of the Hindu or the Champa Kingdom where the visitors may see for themselves how it had spread across the Central Vietnam.

Some of the artifacts that are on display in the Museum are amazing in their scale and size. Notable among those are the four main pedestals - the Tra Kieu Ramayana pedestal, the Tra Kieu 'Apsara' pedestal, the My Son pedestal and the Dong Dunong Buddhist pedestal that represent the extraordinary genius and skill of the craftsmen of the Cham or Champa civilization, ranking them as masterpieces of art by historians across the world.

The Tra Kieu Ramayana Altar celebrates the creative power of 'Lord Shiva' symbolized by the gigantic 'Yoni' and the 'Linga' carved out of sandstone. Such a huge structure of the 'Linga' and the 'Yoni' are rarely found in any of the Hindu temples in India. The base of the pedestal has about four different events from the Ramayana carved around it with about 91 characters that tell the story of the life of Lord Rama. The pedestal depicts gorgeous 'Apsaras' wearing

Square base Linga Pedestal of 10th Century at Da Nang Museum of Cham Sculptures.

ornate jewellery and dancing in celebration during the wedding ceremony of Rama and Sita.

The second masterpiece is the My Son E-l Altar belonging to the 7th and 8th centuries and is considered to exemplify the best of South-East Asian craftsmanship. Carved in a vivid style the pedestal depicts the various activities carried out by the monks of that time, curing illnesses using amulets and massages. The carving includes figures of several animals like parrots, monkeys, tigers and wild pigs in thick forests where the Hindu monks are shown praying, meditating, preaching or celebrating life by singing and dancing. The main figures are seen leaning gracefully, holding a silk band of cloth.

The Dong Dunong pedestal belongs to the 9th and 10th centuries, highlighting the genius of the Cham craftsmen. A collection from the Buddhist sanctuaries, the carvings depict the stories from Buddha Sakyamuni's life. The faces of the statues of the Champa Kings have an indigenous look, showing them with big eyes, nose and thick lips. It showcases that period of the Champa kingdom when Buddhism was the dominant religion.

The Tra Kien 'Apsara' pedestal that was carved probably by the end of 10th century depicts a magnificent 'Apsara' as the main dancing figure and leaning in front of a lotus. It is a remarkable piece of art for its elegance and grace and immortalizes the female beauty in stone.

Apart from the aforesaid four main pedestals, there is a huge pedestal depicting seven 'Lingas' of Lord Shiva-together. Besides there are several large and not so large statues of Lord Shiva showing him with flowing locks of hair and dancing (the 'Nataraj') etc. There are vivid carvings of myriad deities like Lord Vishnu, Indra with 'Apsaras' dancing around him, goddess of learning Saraswati, Parvati - the consort of Lord Shiva and her son Lord Ganesha, goddess of wealth Lakshmi, Bhagavati and the Yaksha. Accompanying these main deities there are several large and smaller statues of animals like elephants, lions, sea-monsters, the predatory bird 'Garuda' devouring a snake etc, which are placed in the outer precincts of the temple towers and these stand guard to the gods and goddesses inside. The museum also has on display several altars, idols and other decorative works that have been collected from various Hindu and Buddhist sanctuaries from all over central Vietnam. It is amazing to note that the figures of the deities as also the human figures carved around the main deity bear a strong resemblance to the figures that one finds in the Indian temples and which indicate that these sculptures might have been sculpted by Indian artisans and craftsmen.

The museum has also on display large photographs on the first floor showing the celebration of Kate Festival at the temple-towers, which is still celebrated in its traditional form on the 1st of July of the Cham Saka Calendar. Through these photographs the visitors to the Museum may have some idea of the vibrance and vitality of the Cham culture. During this festival the Cham community gathers in large numbers wearing their traditional dresses and colourful headgears and playing their traditional musical instruments like drums and cymbals etc. for three days; festivity of religious prayers and rituals accompanied by dancing, singing and feasting together. The museum has human sized mannequins wearing the traditional dresses. The traditional musical instruments are encased in glass cases, categorized with details about the various material used in their construction and their respective importance in the musical orchestra during the celebrations.

There is also a bronze statue belonging to the Cham period in the Cham Museum. This 1.20m. high statue of 'Avalokiteshvara' or 'Tara' holding a lotus and a conch in either hands belongs to the 9th Century and is said to be discovered accidentally by a farmer in Quang Nam province. Since it is the most precious relic of the past, a replica of this statue has been put up in the museum for security reasons. The original one is taken out for display on certain very special occasions.

While visiting the Da Nang Museum of Cham Sculptures at Da Nang, I was taken to a gift sale counter that sold various souvenirs, handicrafts, picture post-cards and various other Cham art works. I was surprised to find that souvenirs included had crafted ladies bags, purses, embroidered pieces of attires that were almost identical to the ones available at handicraft shops of Puri, (in the state of Odisha), in India. I was amazed to see the Cham handicrafts and its striking similarity with those of India. It was an overwhelming experience for me.

The museum is a remarkable confluence of the past and the present. Experts and archaeologists are constantly engaged in carrying out researches. Books and papers are also regularly published from this museum. Even foreigners, who are interested in research and exploration of this rich ancient cultural heritage are also welcome here. We spent three fruitful days of our research work with the help and guidance of the director of the museum Vo Van Thang, who is an erudite and co-operative person.

The Director of Da Nang Museum of Cham Sculptures or the Champa Museum, Mr. Vo Van Thang, is a very lively and

Author with Prof. Vo Van Thang, Directer Da Nang Museurn of Cham Scupture at the office of the Museum.

knowledgeable person and he also happens to be the President of Da Nang - India Friendship Association. In our private conversation he informed that every year around 300,000 visitors from various parts of the world visit the Champa Museum but it is an irony that the number of Indian visitors is hardly two to three hundred every year.

The museum is one of the biggest and unique of its kind in the world where thousands of artifacts, sculptures, rock inscriptions and steles depicting Hindu religion and culture are on display and which provide an insight to the viewers about the development and expansion of the Hindu kingdom and religion in Vietnam. It also enlightens the viewer about the deep impression and influence of India over the Vietnamese society. In Fact, Da Nang is the centre wherefrom one may have glimpses of ancient history of Hindu kingdoms, Hindu religion and Hindu culture, that dominated the central part of Vietnam for 15 centuries.

In fact, despite Vietnam being a household name in India, especially in West Bengal, the people in India are almost ignorant about this aspect of their past cultural links with Vietnam.

Who is to be blamed for this shortcoming?

Our very own Government, in spite of having most cordial relations with Vietnam failed to highlight this historical aspect of mutual relations that binds the two countries in a common bond.

The Government of Vietnam is also to be blamed to certain extent as it also was found lacking to highlight the aforesaid aspect in the light of the impact of the Hindu Brahmanical culture and kept believing and propagating the Cham culture, which happens to be none other than the Hindu or Brahmanical culture. Had the government of Vietnam highlighted the Cham temple towers as Hindu temples, it would have naturally attracted Hindu or Indian visitors to tour those sites to track their past cultural links. Then naturally besides increasing tourist traffic to Vietnam it would also have boosted the bilateral relations between the two peoples of India and Vietnam.

16

CU CHI TUNNEL : A TESTIMONY OF STRENGTH OF HUMAN WILL

Cu Chi Tunnel situated about 70 kms. north west of Ho Chi Minh City in South Vietnam had added a glorious chapter in the liberation war of Vietnam earlier against the French colonialists and later against the US imperialists. Today among the war memorials in Vietnam it has become one of the most important destinations for the war tourism. This tunnel carried a greater significance for me as during the Liberation War or The American War, I was emotionally involved with the Liberation War of Vietnam against the US imperialists. I had participated in a number

Author coming out from the Cu Chi tunnel.

Author at Cu Chi Tunnel.

of rallies, processions and demonstrations organised in Calcutta (now Kolkata) against the US high handedness in Vietnam and had heard a lot of tales about the heroic deeds of the Vietnamese guerillas in their resistance against the American forces. Naturally, when in 1982 I visited Ho Chi Minh City for the first time in an Indian delegation, our visit to Cu Chi Tunnel formed a prominent part of our itinerary. The journey to the tunnel was a bit difficult and not as comfortable as it is now.

Thereafter, whenever I visited Ho Chi Minh City, I made it a point to pay my salutations to the valiant guerillas of Vietnam's liberation war through my visit to Cu Chi Tunnel.

In 2015 also, when on our initiative Ms. Smita Pant, the Hon'ble Consul General of India in Ho Chi Minh City had organized an exhibition from 31st August to 3rd September 2015 at the War Remnants Museum to mark the occasion of 40th Anniversary of the Victory of Liberation War and Unification of Vietnam, myself and my Colleagues Kusum Jain and Pravamayee Samantaray not only participated in the function but despite tight schedule we visited this tunnel to pay our tributes to the heroic freedom fighters of Vietnam, who had sacrificed their lives for the liberation of their nation.

It was built during a long period of about 25 years, beginning sometime in the late 1940s probably from 1947 onwards during Vietnam's war against the French. The special thing of the construction of this tunnel was that the guerrillas continued their fight against the enemy from these tunnels that were used as their hideouts and simultaneously carried on with their task of construction.

The network of the tunnel stretched from the then Saigon to the border of Cambodia, a total distance of about 250 kms. that the guerillas and local peasants manually dug by their hands without using any equipment to ensure that nobody could guess what was going on under the ground.

As mentioned above, the construction took around 25 long years and at least two generations worked and fought in the tunnel. During such a long period the enemy did not get a hint of it. Their spying network failed to manage even a single informer. French or American did not find a single man or woman in Vietnam, who could betray to his or her Fatherland Front – a rare example of patriotism! At least 45,000 Vietnamese men and women died defending the Cu Chi tunnels.

The tunnels had four levels for different purposes. The top level had traps, ventilation shafts and firing posts while the second level had kitchen and sleeping chambers. The third level housed the Aid Station for the wounded, a storage for weapons and food stuffs, and a route connected to the tunnel systems. The fourth and the last level had a well for water. It was quite hard for the Americans to discover these areas due to numerous deceptive routes in the tunnels leading nowhere.

The tunnels were too complex and confusing for the Americans and to add to their woes the guerrillas set many tricks inside and outside the tunnels. Inside they created fake tunnels' routes so as to lead the Americans to either dead end or to booby traps. There had been various traps outside the tunnels too to mislead the enemy.

Being baffled by the strategy of sudden outbursts of the guerillas from nowhere, the Americans began deploying German Shepherd dogs trained to use their keen smelling sense to locate the trap doors and the guerillas. The guerillas in the tunnel were a step ahead and responded by washing themselves with American soaps that gave off a scent, the canines identified as friendly. To confuse the dog squads further, the uniforms of the captured US soldiers were put out, and in the process so many dogs were killed or maimed that their frightened handlers refused to send them to the tunnels anymore.

Life in the tunnel was extremely difficult and suffocating. There were scarcity of air, water, food and light. Tunnels were infested with ants, mosquitoes, poisonous centipedes, scorpions, spiders and vermin. Some times during heavy bombing, guerillas were forced to remain underground for many days. Sickness was rampant especially malaria, which was the second largest cause of death among the people living in the tunnels.

Meanwhile, by the late 1960s the Americans began carpet bombing the Cu Chi Tunnels area thereby destroying several portions of it, but by then the US was already on its way out of the war and the tunnels had already served their purpose.

When the National Liberation Front insurgency began around 1960, the old tunnels were repaired and new extensions were excavated. Within a few years the tunnel system assumed enormous strategic importance and most of the Cu Chi district and its nearing areas came under firm control of the guerrillas.

The 250 kms. long complex of Cu Chi Tunnels has since been preserved and turned into a war memorial park. The tunnels are now a popular tourist attraction where visitors are taken down the memory lane to crawl around in the safer parts of the tunnel systems. Some tunnels have been made larger to accommodate the western tourists while low power lights have been installed in several of them to make travelling through them easier and booby traps have been clearly marked.

A model of village scene displayed at Cu Chi Tunnel.

The Cu Chi Tunnels are, in fact, a powerful testimony to the strength of the human will against overwhelming odds.

This time my colleague Pravamayee Samantaray was with us. It was her first visit to Cu Chi Tunnel. Our guide quizzed her if she could locate any trap-door nearby? She tried to locate but could not and accepted defeat. Finally, he lifted a wooden plank just right before her feet. It was a trap with spear like pointed bamboo sticks. A fall could have proved fatal. The Vietnamese sharp shooting guerrillas used to hide in the camouflaged 'spider hole' dugouts.

We also visited those rooms and enclosures that were reserved for the education of the children. It clearly indicated the extent of importance that was provided to education. We also witnessed the conference rooms where war strategies were formulated.

Our guide explained to us the operational methods of the Vietnamese guerrillas, who appeared from nowhere like lightning and disappeared within seconds after striking the target. The guerilla soldiers continued with their guerilla warfare for years.

Last leg of our visit to the tunnel was the replica of an underground

At the small outdoor workshop near Cu Chi Tunnel gate. An instructor demonstrating to visitors how to make 'Ho Chi Minh Sandals'.

kitchen-cum-canteen. Our guide offered us a sample of steamed manioc with grinded peanuts, which we enjoyed as we were hungry.

Outside the gate to the tunnels, there are refreshment and souvenir kiosks where one can find from snake wine (rice liqueur marinating baby cobras and green snakes in bottles, whose labels promise potent curative powers) to ball point pens made from bullets.

Near the Cu Chi Tunnel gate there is a small outdoor workshop where instructors offer a crash course to the visitors in making 'Ho Chi Minh Sandals'. It is done with rubber harvested from bleeding trees on the spot.

After our guided tour to the tunnel we were shown an interesting documentary film about the Cu Chi Tunnel.

To attract the tourist traffic from all over the world, the government of Vietnam has expanded the area of Cu Chi Tunnel and has extended it to many more hectares, where live shows depicting the underground classes to educate the children and peasants working in the field during nights, women stitching uniforms for the guerillas, people carrying out various day to day activities, are held.

In the complex of the Cu Chi War Memorial there is a beautiful big man-made lake around which there are a number of eateries and restaurants. In one of those restaurants we had our lunch and departed.

17

AMAZING TEMPLES

We stayed in Ben Tre for two days. On the first day after having our lunch we were told that we will be taken to some famous temples. Temples? It was quite surprising for us that we will be taken to certain temples and that too in Vietnam.

The temple we visited in Ben Tre was quite peculiar. It looked like a pagoda with steep horned roof spiking the sky. The idol in the sanctum of the temple was neither of Buddha nor of any other deity. When we asked the name of the deity our Vietnamese

A view of the temple of blind poet Nguyen Dinh Chieu.

friends crammed incense sticks in our hands and said that the idol was that of Nguyen Dinh Chieu. We were startled for a moment and then remembered that it was the name of a poet, whose bust we had seen in the Vietnam Writers' Museum and who had lost his eye sight while wailing and crying in the memory of his deceased mother. When we told this to our Vietnamese friends they confirmed that it was the temple of that said blind poet.

We wondered. The existence of the bust of the poet and his photograph in the Writers' Museum was nothing unusual to us, but to have a huge idol of the same blind poet installed in the sanctum at the place of a deity was a matter of surprise for us. However, suppressing our surprise we wanted to know about the main idol and various figures carved over black stones on the wall. Ao Dai, our charming guide, who was in traditional Vietnamese dress, informed us with a sense of glory that Nguyen Dinh Chieu (1822-1888) was a great poet of the province, who had written a biographical epic titled 'Luc Van Tien' and was as popular among the people as epic 'Kim and Kieu'? written by Nguyen Du (1766-1820).

In his 'Funeral Oration for Can Giuoc Partisans' the poet Nguyen Dinh Chieu had written a narrative poem about the simple and patriotic cultivators, who had fought against the French colonialists with most non-conventional weapons like wooden spears and javelins bare footed, wearing tattered garments.

Nguyen Dinh Chieu came of a low ranking mandarin family and was educated in Hue where while preparing to sit for his Bachelor's Degree examination, he got the news of his mother's death. Naturally, he had to abandon his examination and proceed to his home. He was extremely attached to his mother and so on her death he wailed and cried to such an extent that he lost his eye-sight and that was the end of his academic career. In his native place Can Giuoc, he opened a school to teach about traditional medicines but when the area was wrested by the French, in 1962 he came to settle in Ben Tre province situated on the Mekong Delta, where he lived for about 26 years till his death. He had seven children. Whatever he dictated was put in writing earlier by his wife and later by his daughter, who was his fifth child. The most distinguishing part of his writing is that he wrote in the most simple language which even a layman could comprehend. The poet despised the French and everything that was French like camera etc. It is for this reason that there is no photograph of his available. The photograph that is available is made out from that of his seventh son who was carbon copy of his father, by blinding his eyes.

This temple of Nguyen Dinh Chieu will always be etched in our memory since it was the temple of a great poet.

Our next halt was at another temple - Nguyen Thi Dinh Temple. Once again we were amazingly surprised to find an idol of a woman in the sanctum instead of any deity. Who was this simple woman having no halo around her like most of the deities? We wondered, who was this woman, who earned so much of reverence and devotion of the people that they not only built a temple dedicated to her but who worship and adore her also with great esteem? Our guide, the young Vietnamese girl in traditional attire informed us that the idol in the sanctum was that of a patriotic revolutionary Vietnamese woman named Nguyen Thi Dinh, who had led the insurrection against the French colonial regime in Ben Tre province in 1945 and then again against the U.S. backed Diem regime in 1960.

This outstanding valiant revolutionary lady Nguyen Thi Dinh was born on 15th March, 1920 in Luong Hoa village of Giong Taom district in Ben Tre province. She was born in a family known to be engaged in struggle against the colonial regime. Her brother Ba Chan was arrested and imprisoned by the 'puppet' village officials, who were governing on behalf of the French, in suspicion of underground activities. Dinh being the youngest of the family used to carry food for her imprisoned brother everyday and witnessed the sense of brutality over young and old inmates alike in the prison by the officials. Naturally, such scenes enraged her to

A view of Nguyen Thi Dinh Temple.

such an extent that even at a tender age she decided to become a revolutionary. She wrote in her memoirs that for her 'there was no other road to take'.

When she grew her parents put pressure on her to get married but she reluctantly replied that she was a revolutionary and would marry only a revolutionary, who would never object to her revolutionary activities. Subsequently, when she was 17, she had an occasion to meet a friend of her brother, a famous intellectual and revolutionary, Bich Thuan, whom she married in 1938. In 1940, when her son was only three days old, the soldiers of the 'puppet' regime arrested her husband and deported him to French prison at French island Puolo Condore, where he died on 12th July 1942.

Meanwhile, in 1940 itself when her son was barely seven months old, she was also arrested and sent to Ba Ra, a prison near the Cambodian border. By the end of 1943 when she was suffering from cardiac ailment, she was sent back home and kept under house arrest. In 1945 she led a massive crowd of thousands of people of Ben Tre armed with knives, sticks, flags, bright red banners and placards and seized the power from the French authorities in Ben Tre. After the successful uprising in Ben Tre in 1945, she was assigned to work at the village and district levels to organise women's network and unite them and with utmost sincerity she executed the job assigned to her. In 1945 she got married for the second time to her second husband Nguyen Huu Tri.

In 1946 she was chosen by the Province Party Committee to travel with other delegates to the North to meet President Ho Chi Minh and to request him to provide weapons for the struggle in the South. Although Ho granted their request but asked them to seize more weapons from the French to continue their fight well against the French. She was hardly 26 then when she loaded the weapons onto a small boat along with two 50 years old men and two youths and despite French naval blockade, smuggled them to the South. This one act demonstrated her gallant and brave endeavours.

In 1960 National Liberation Front, a Southern mass organization with communists at its core was founded which was called 'Vietcong'. Nguyen Thi Dinh served as its important representative at a rally that was held at Ben Tre province and organized many battalions of women, 'long haired' troops dedicated to political struggle. As the deputy commander of the South Vietnam Liberation Forces, she continued to organise women in villages and hamlets. In due course of time she became famous as the 'General of the Long Haired Army'. The women members of the Long Haired Army specialised in commando operations, reconnaissance, communication and nursing etc.

From 1965 to 1974 she was the Deputy Commander of South Vietnam Liberation Front and on 1st April 1974 she became the first woman General of the Army and during that war in Mekong Delta General Nguyen Thi Dinh led the People's Liberation Armed Force (NLAF).

In 1982 she became the President of Vietnam Women's Union and for next ten years she devoted herself towards establishing Women's Union in every village, district and province.

Nguyen Thi Dinh was so dare devil that she had several encounters with death but every time she somehow or other survived and kept on inspiring her fellows for more dare devil acts. However, finally on 26th August 1992 she breathed her last in Ho Chi Minh City.

We had earlier seen the statues, busts of various national heroes installed at prominent places in various countries of the world. Various roads and avenues have been named after their names to commemorate their deeds and heroism. However, this was the first instance when we found a temple built to commemorate a valiant, indomitable and heroic woman patriot who is not only being remembered with reverence by her fellow countrymen but who is also worshipped by them. We were literally overwhelmed to visit this unique temple.

18

A TRUE SECULAR COUNTRY

Vietnam, as I have observed during my numerous visits, is a deeply religious country.

Deeply religious?

Yes, of course. The people of Vietnam, in general, love and enjoy festivals and so in the garb of religion they add few more festivals and have their share of enjoyment.

The majority of the people in Vietnam are the followers of Buddhism, followed by Confucianism, Taoism and Christianity besides the 54 ethnic groups, who follow their own faiths.

As per census the majority of population in Vietnam has declared themselves to be the humanists and not religious. This is an amazing contradiction that exists in the Vietnamese society that although every one enjoys religious festivals, yet majority of them are humanists by faith.

According to the constitution of Vietnam, every citizen enjoys the right to observe or not to observe any religion. However, one thing that deserves mention here is that there is no public holiday on the basis of the religion.

Every religious society needs to be registered with the government in Vietnam according to the constitution and has to submit its annual statement of accounts to the concerned authorities.

Basically, the land in Vietnam belongs to the state and so, for the purpose of development, the government is free to acquire even a religious property and to allot an alternate place for it.

I do not remember the exact year but I still do remember that in a suburb of Ho Chi Minh City an ancient Pagoda was being relocated. It was amazing and surprising for me as I was unaware of this technology of relocating the whole structure from one place to another.

I had also witnessed a Ganesha Temple in the old Ho Chi Minh City being demolished to widen the street without any hue and cry. This goes on to prove that the people love development still more than the religion.

In Vietnam the Constitution enjoys the supreme place followed by the nation and its people. However, in the interest of the people, the constitution is amended from time to time and so it may finally be deduced that ultimately the people are supreme.

During my various visits to Vietnam, I had the occasion to visit several religious places that included pagodas, churches, mosques, particularly the Indian Moske built by Indian Muslims in Ho Chi Minh City, besides several ancient Hindu temples dating back from seventh to fourteenth century scattered in central Vietnam from Phan Tiet to My Son and Hoi An, and of course around the centuries' old Hindu temples in Ho Chi Minh City and as I observed everywhere that the religious groups enjoyed their religious liberties, of course while abiding by the rules of the land. I may name a few religious festivals here that are quite local in nature viz. the Huong Pagoda Festival, the Yen Tu Pagoda Festival, the Phu Giay Festival, the Thay Pagoda Festival, the Lang Pagoda Festival, the Hon Chen Temple Festival, the Thap Ba Festival etc. The list is too long and may take volumes if I mention them all.

As mentioned earlier, every ethnic group in Vietnam has its own religion that is followed and observed by its thousand to 3-4 hundred thousand followers. There are many religions that are confined to certain distant villages in the mountainous or highland areas of Vietnam.

No TV Channel in Vietnam ever propagates superstition or religion. Yet, I believe, the Vietnamese are superstitious to certain extent as they pray to God, to Lord Buddha for their welfare, better future, better services and so on, although they seem to be aware that they are the masters of their own destiny and that no other power has any control over their future. There are a few fortune tellers in Vietnam to whom a person visits when deeply distressed to find out some sort of remedy to one's distress.

I asked my Vietnamese friend if there was any hate campaign in the social media against any particular religion or religious belief, the point blank answer was 'No'.

The Government and the administration in Vietnam does not at all interfere in the day to day rituals of the religions, however, it does take care that rules of the land are observed and not violated. If any religious ritual is contrary to the mental, spiritual and material development, the Government comes forward to educate the people to change in accordance with the time.

It needs no mention that Vietnam is a Buddhist country and its every town, city or village has at least one Buddhist Pagoda and monks serving in those. There are some ancient pagodas that date back hundreds of years besides new magnificent pagodas, that are coming up, financed mostly by non-resident rich Vietnamese settled abroad. However, Buddhism is not a state religion as the state follows secular lines.

There are many cults of Buddhism. During some of my last visits, I observed that 'Therevada Buddhism' was taking upperhand. According to historians Therevada Buddhism went to Vietnam directly from India when during the first century or may be even earlier some monks had travelled to Vietnam to propagate Buddhism.

In the northern part of Vietnam China ruled from 1st to 10th century. They also, later on, brought the Chinese version of Buddhism, Mahayana besides Confucianism and Taoism.

In recent years, I found that the religions brought by China are losing their space among the Vietnamese followers and the Therevada cult is gaining followers. Meanwhile local Buddhist cults are also emerging with small followings.

This trend of Therevada Buddhism has become the strongest friendly bond between India and Vietnam and it would gain momentum and importance in days to come.

19

VIETNAM WRITERS' UNION AND MUSEUM

Vietnam Writers' Union has been an association in Vietnam that has all along been playing an important role and has been active in promoting, uniting and assembling the world fraternity of writers and literators over one platform through its numerous seminars, workshops and other functions that it organises from time to time. Even I had the honour of participating in its five international seminars and workshops, and I was pleasantly surprised to observe that in those international seminars and workshops besides hundreds of Vietnamese writers, writers from about 25 to 40 nations including China had participated.

In one such international gathering while chatting and interacting with Chinese delegates, I lightly remarked - "Comrade, here we are meeting and participating in various functions in a friendly and family atmosphere. Why can't we behave likewise on other fronts as well?" The Chinese delegate smilingly said, "here we should abstain from politics." It was obvious that he was reluctant to discuss on the issue.

The credit for the record of activities of Vietnam Writers' Union for past several years should go to its President poet Huu Thinh, who has been instrumental in collecting resources through government sources and organising activities on such a wide scale. Since last three-four years, however, since the government has also curtailed the funds drastically, so the activities have also been curtailed as a result.

Besides being a powerful people's poet Huu Thinh had been a committed freedom fighter who had actively participated in Vietnam's liberation war with gun in one hand and pen in the other.

It was due to the initiative of Huu Thinh that Vietnam Writers' Union could have a magnificent building of its own and a guest house with about a dozen guest-rooms besides about five small and big seminar halls, and a lobby.

Vietnamese writers are continuing with their legacy and are writing powerful pieces of literature even today. Poets outnumber the prose writers. Every poet craves to have at least one collection of his poems published and when published they share the publication with their fellow writers and earn their appreciation in return. The matter of concern is that the readership of literary pieces has alarmingly decreased although the number of writers has not declined.

Quite near the offices and the Guest House of Vietnam Writers' Union, a newly built seven storeyed building has come up which is known as Vietnam Writers' Museum. The initiative of building such a museum was made in 1995 but for various reasons its construction could not begin till 2004.

Poet Huu Thinh, who is also the director of the museum informed us that the museum was a proper place to recognise the great writers and their literary works. He also informed us that during the under-construction period of ten years of the museum they had received huge amount of contributions of objects and materials of the great writers of Vietnam. We were told that the museum possessed more than 40,000 objects and materials on about a thousand writers of the country but due to limited space available only about 3,500 objects and materials are on display.

One floor of the museum has on display the typical works representing literature from the 10th to the 19th centuries. The works are on various materials like paper, cloth, metal and leaves. There are also works by great writers of the feudal period such as King Tran Nhan Tong (1258-1308), Nguyen Trai (1380-1442) and Nguyen Du (1766-1820). Nguyen Du's epic poem titled 'Kim & Kieu' (The Tale of Kieu) is also on display along with some of its foreign language translations.

Another floor of the museum is reserved for the writers of the anti-French revolution period (1945-1954), while one more floor has on display the works of foreign authors on and about Vietnamese writers and literature. This floor also has on display the busts of Alexander Pushkin and Rabindranath Tagore.

Another floor named 'Folklore Hall' is dedicated to the folklore of Vietnam while the seventh top floor of the museum has a number of meetings and conference halls.

On the top floor of the museum there is a lively exhibition of Vietnam as it was about seventy, eighty years back where through mannequins it has been shown how oil was extracted from the oil-seeds, how the cultivators ploughed the field, how the wood was used as a fuel, how the agricultural equipments were made with the use of bellows, how the people gossiped around camp fires. I thought I was witnessing the scenes that I used to see in my village in India during my childhood.

Vietnam Writers' Museum has, in fact, enlivened more than thousand years' old cultural and literary heritage of Vietnam. It has preserved manuscripts of old and modern writers on display along with the biographies and about fifty busts of prominent writers. Besides busts and manuscripts of some writers, their belongings viz. their table, chairs, pens, ink-pots, their typewriters and attires are also principal attraction for the viewers. At certain places some lively shows are also organised with the help of cinematography and modern technology. The museum also allows visitors to use modern computer software to search for more information about writers.

Author With Poet Huu Thinh Director, Vietnam Writers' Museum inside the museum hall.

This visit of ours to the Vietnam Writers' Museum halls in the museum took place where ten to fifty tourists, visitors or writers may have an intimate dialogue and interaction over a cup of coffee. Needless to say that such dialogues and interactions are quite effective to unite the people and promote a sense of world fraternity among them.

We spent about four hours in the museum and still we wished to have some more time at our hand.

20

TET : A FESTIVAL OF JOY, LOVE AND COMPASSION

The basic character of Vietnamese civilization, its society and its people, by and large, is secular. Vietnam is a country of festivals. Almost every day a festival takes place in one corner or another in Vietnam. Festivals exist as a break from the regular routine, and as a unifying force within communities. It is amazing to witness that most of the festivals have nothing to do with religion. Sometimes the festivals are based on mythological stories.

TET is the biggest festival of Vietnam. It takes place between 20th January and 10th February as per lunar calendar. People pay tribute to their ancestors and martyrs, who sacrificed their lives to liberate their fatherland from foreign aggressors. People are so deeply involved with the festivals that one of the greatest peasant leaders of Vietnam, Quang Trung, asked his soldiers to celebrate the festival first before attacking the Manchu invaders, who had come up to Hanoi.

For three days and sometime five days, when it occurs just before or after the weekends, people go crazy, forgetting their misery, sorrow, enmity and all sorts of worries. They rejoice each and every moment of the festival, meeting family members and friends, exchanging gifts, embracing each other and loving one and all. It is also amazing that at least for this period they get rid of all sorts of anger or enmity and try to help each other.

From children to old people, men, women, old and young everybody without exception rejoice, rejoice and only rejoice. Even during the festival a rude mother-in-law also treats her daughter-in-law affectionately. A quarrelsome couple faces each other with smile. People behave finely and lovingly expecting good health, happiness and prosperity in the year ahead. According to Vietnamese custom, the actions during these days would be followed by the twelve months ahead. With the end of holidays, Vietnamese resume their respective work with new zeal.

There are many stories behind this festival, but one is very famous and widely accepted. The story goes like this:

"A couple was very much in love. Alas, they were childless and so the conjugal harmony suffered. One day, after a quarrel, the wife left her husband, whose name was Trong Cao, and went away to another region, where she married. Her new husband, Pham Lang, loved her dearly.

After a long time spent in solitude and sorrow, Trong Cao went in search of his wife Thi Nhi. He spent all that he had, and eventually had to beg for a living. By chance, he came to the house of Pham Lang, who was that day at work in the fields. Thi Nhi gave him a good meal. She had recognized him, while he, who had grown partly blind because of hunger and illness, failed to see in her his former wife. Having drunk some wine, he fell into a slumber. Thi Nhi took him into the courtyard and hid him under a heap of straw to avoid facing embarrassing questions when Pham Lang returned. In the late afternoon, back from the fields, her husband set fire to the heap of dried straw in order to make fertilizer from the ashes. Before Thi Nhi could intervene, Trong Cao had been burnt to death. Wild with sorrow, she threw herself into the flames. In his turn, driven by despair, Pham Lang also jumped into the raging fire. The Emperor of Heaven, moved by the genuine feeling uniting the three people, made them into household gods. The Vietnamese version, born of a tragedy of love, faithfulness and sacrifice, touches the heart more deeply."

Above mentioned story reminds one the Greek tragedy that leaves a deep scar on hearts. Nobody knows how this Greek tragedy is converted in most joyful event of the life. Relatives and acquaintances not only from Vietnam but abroad also wait for the TET and they make it a point to visit their country from every part of the world where they have settled and of course, from every corner of Vietnam.

People decorate their houses inside and outside, prepare best cuisine, particularly sweets. They prepare a particular type of sweet made up of rice and sugar, wrapped in banana leaves. Another special cuisine prepared during TET is Banh Chung. It is a square rice cake stuffed with fat pork, beans and shallots. The square shape is symbolic of mother earth. Betel has a very pious and religious significance as it is offered to ancestors during TET.

Whatever cuisine they prepare, they not only take themselves, but present it to friends, neighbours and relatives. It is a community festival, which involves each and every citizen irrespective of religions.

I do not remember the exact period, but I was in Vietnam once on the occasion of TET festival and enjoyed the festival like any Vietnamese forgetting my homeland. I also witnessed that foreigner who happens to be in Vietnam on the occasion of TET enjoys each and every moment assimilating himself with the festivity.

As mentioned earlier, this festival has nothing to do with the religion, people pay tribute to their ancestors. They repair if necessary and decorate the ancestors' graves before the festival. Every house in Vietnam has a small place, like a temple, where portraits or photos of their ancestors are placed and worshipped, instead of god or goddess. Ancestors are invited to return and share their merry making. Throughout the day they offer incense sticks, food, fresh water, flowers and betel to them. This festival is unique of its kind, cannot be compared with any other festival in any part of the world.

This is a festival that the Vietnamese love to share in common and with mutual love; one of the most humanistic festivals in the world. It is humanistic in true sense because it unites man with nature (devotion of farmers to their cultivation), living with the dead (love and respect for the ancestors) and above all it gives an opportunity wherein family members of distant places get together, in-laws specially mother-in-laws and daughter-in-laws come closer by reconciliation, neighbours forgetting their differences do a fresh start etc.

Even during the liberation war, people did not forget to celebrate this festival.

To sum up, it may be said that this festival is purely of human nature depicting love, affection and compassion.

21

A LAND OF ART AND ARTISTS

Vietnamese are great art lovers. I visited their apartments, houses, lived in hotels both small or big, had dinner and lunch at various restaurants and found varieties of interior decorations with tradional crafts and modern paintings. It included paintings on walls, even the doors of elevators were also painted.

Portrait of legendary Poet Nguyen Trai (1382-1442). A Silk craft on display at Vietnam National Museum.

The author and his colleagues with Mr. Tran Khanh Chuong. President of Vietnam Fine Art Association and a host of Vietnamese painters.

Vietnamese traditional arts and crafts are embedded in its culture and in its way of life. It ranges from wood-carving, lacquer-weaving, silver-work, silk painting, basket-weaving etc. in Hanoi, old quarters of 36 streets are named on these traditional crafts such as Hang Bac, engaged in silver making crafts, Hang Quatt means Fan making, Hang Dong means bronze casting. It goes on with other crafts. The word Hang means craft. Toady all these traditional art forms have been revived and given a modern face through new subjects. Artists have experimented with different material and techniques in their traditional art form. One specific quality is that most of the crafts have craft villages.

In cities with some exception, there are some specific areas where artists live and have their workshops at either the ground floor or the first floor. I witnessed many painting exhibitions, art galleries in Hanoi and Ho Chi Minh City. I had the honour to inaugurate an art exhibition organized at Vietnam Fine Art Association, Hanoi. One of the participant painters, Nguyen Khac Chinh had invited us and escorted us to the exhibition. This writer had a long interaction with the President of the Association, Tran Khanh Chuong and was enriched about the painters and paintings of Vietnam.

The painters have a good market, not only in Vietnam, their home country, but they export a big number of paintings to Europe and America. Off and on they are invited to organize their exhibitions and some time to participate in international exhibitions and are rewarded, particularly in France and USA. In recent years, the international art market has seen influx of art works from Vietnam. Exhibitions of contemporary Vietnamese paintings in galleries and museums in New York, California, Asutralia, Hong kong, Japan and Singapore as well as highly profiled auctions house Sotheby's and Christie's have placed Vietnamese paintings on the map of art world.

Most of the artists are whole timers and art is their profession. They earn good money to sustain a comfortable life. Many painters have their ownership flats and cars. Most of them have their workshops at their own flats; they either use a portion of their flats as their workshop or one floor. They teach painting to the desiring aspirants and take affordable fees from them which vary from student to student according to their economic status, but if any aspirant is

A Contemporary paiting.

A Contemporary paiting.

monetarily week, they do not charge. Pravamayee Samantaray, who herself is a painter under training while teaching English in Diplomatic Academy of Vietnam was eager to learn Vietnamese style of painting and requested a painter, Nguyễn Đức Hùng to learn from him. He not only readily agreed, but told that as she was from a friendly country, 'Ấn Độ' (India in Vietnamese) so he would not charge anything from her. I visited Vietnam University of Fine Arts, Hanoi situated in a multi storied building and a vast area around. Outside the campus, there were many shops which were selling basic materials for painting and a few paintings also. I also visited many painters' houses, who were most hospitable.

One sculpturist, Điêu Khắc Liên Vũ runs a restaurant. In a part of the restaurant he has displayed his sculptures of various sizes and does brisk business in the restaurant besides selling sculptures, mostly to the foreign tourists.

I take pride to mention that on the occasion of Kolkata International Book Fair 2015, which is biggest in the world as far as peoples' participation is concerned, we had invited a few painters to exhibit their paintings in 'Vietnam Pavilion' in the book fair. Those were highly appreciated by the Indian viewers. The painters who had come on our invitation were- Nguyen Khac Chinh, Nguyễn Đức Hùng, Tao Huong, Lan Echo, Phạm Huy Hùng.

2016 was a year of plentiful offerings in the secondary market for Vietnamese modern art. Auctions in France and the US — increasingly accessible to buyers in Asia via online marketing and sales platforms - turned up more Vietnamese artworks than previous years (with accompanying strong prices) against a backdrop of strong prices in the bellwether Hong Kong auction sales. Christie's presented in its May 2016 Asian 20th-Century Art sale a curated section titled 'Se Souvenir des Belles Choses: A Curated Collection of Vietnamese Art' that featured more than 70 Vietnamese lots in its 20th-century Asian art sale. With a 90% sell-through rate, and a sale total of USD 4 million, it was not only the most valuable single auction sale of Vietnamese art but also notable for the overwhelming response of Vietnam-based buyers, who accounted for more than half of the sold value of the sale, in fact, Vietnam's contemporary art is still an untapped goldmine to be discovered on the global market.

Artists at a workshop.

22

FOLKLORE A RICH HERITAGE

I may not be an authority on folklore but I love to read and listen to the folktales. That reminds me of my childhood when I was an apt listener of folktales of various countries that I had the occasion to visit later . Naturally, I have a collection of Vietnamese folktales also.

Folklore are an inbuilt part of Vietnamese culture depicted through customs, festivals, proverbs. They interact with history of Vietnam. They are the legacy of many millennia of human interaction with the land. They implant themselves so deeply in the hearts that they become more than images . They are deeply human and long for happy humane relations.

On my part it is difficult to say which country is richer in folktales – Vietnam or India but one thing is for sure that Vietnam is one of the richest countries in folktales in the world.

I visited dozens of places – Hanoi, Hoi An, Hue, Ben Tre etc. Everywhere I was told some or the other folktale about the existence of certain lakes, about betel leaves, about certain trees, mountain etc. It was a pleasant surprise for me to observe striking similarities of certain Vietnamese and Indian folktales. For research this is a virgin area in India although some research work has already been done in Vietnam in this direction.

There are a number of festivals, including TET that have a folktale behind it.

I am tempted to refer hereunder a folktale published in Heritage 2015, a house magazine of Vietnam Airlines and this folktale "The Cowherd and The Weaver" also is related to a festival in Vietnam, that is observed every year during the 8th month of the year in July as per lunar calendar.

"The Cowherd and The Weaver"

Deep in the woods there once stood a pure spring known as the Fairy Well. Since few humans passed that way, fairies often gathered to fetch water and, took off their wings, to bathe.

One day, a lonely young man went out to collect firewood and got lost. While trying to find his way home, he stumbled upon the Fairy Well. There, three fairies were playing and bathing. Seeing their wings on the ground, the young man took one pair and hid behind a tree.

After their bath, the three fairies went ashore. The first two found their wings and soared away. While the last fairy searched for her wings, the young man stepped out and said: "Please follow me home and be my wife. I will make you happy."

Although the fairy wept and begged, the young man refused to return her wings. Finally, she agreed to follow him home. Back at his house, he carefully hid her wings, then prepared food and clothing for her. In course of time, she agreed to be his wife.

Eventually, the fairy gave birth to a son. The young man was thrilled with his happy boy and pleased that his wife seldom asked for her wings or spoke of returning to heaven.

One day, when the boy was three, the young man had to go away to work. Before leaving, he told his wife: "If you get hungry, please take rice from this jar, not that jar." He then pointed to another jar and said: "And never touch this jar, or else bees will sting you and our son."

But the wife didn't follow her husband's instructions. Having eaten everything in the first jar, she turned to the forbidden jar. Inside lay her wings.

While the fairy longed to visit her parents and sisters, she was worried about leaving her young son. When her husband was due to return she decided it was time to go. She prepared a huge batch of cakes for the boy, then stuck a comb into his pocket and said: "Please keep this comb for your dad." Not long after, she flew away.

Upon his return, the young man was devastated. He became very depressed and his son missed his mother bitterly. One day, the man carried the boy to the Fairy Well and sat down to wait. The following day, an old fairy flew down and the young man approached her and explained his story. "Please ask my wife to fly down to see us for a while," he begged. "This is the comb she left me. Please give it to her."

"I know her," said the old fairy. "She is a Fairy Weaver and she misses you! I will tell her."

The following day, two fairies descended from heaven and threw a rope to the young man. They promised to lift him and his son up to heaven if they would close their eyes and stay silent. The pair were pulled higher and higher. At midnight, they entered the heavenly kingdom. The family reunion was joyful.

But after two days, the man and boy had to leave. The rules were strict: humans could not stay in heaven. Despite her love for her husband and son, the Weaver Fairy could not return to the mortal world. Sadly, she presented her husband with a drum and a jar of rice. "Once you reach the ground, bang on the drum three times and I will cut the rope," she told him. Their descent was slow. By midday, the father and son were only halfway down. Seeing his son cry in hunger, the man poured out some rice to feed him. The hungry boy spilled some rice onto , the drum and a flock of ravens swooped down and pecked at the drum. Up in heaven, the Weaver

Fairy heard the drum beats and thought her husband and son were safely on the ground. She cut the rope and the pair fell into the sea.

Realizing they were to blame for this tragedy, the ravens flew to heaven crying loudly. The Heavenly Emperor took pity on the family and turned the young man and his son into heavenly cowherds. They were ordered to graze their buffaloes on one side of the Milky Way. On the other side, the Weaver Fairy worked diligently. Each year, on Lunar July 7, the ravens were commanded to build a bridge across the Milky Way so that the family could briefly reunite.

Since then, it usually rains on Lunar July 7th. The raindrops are the tears of this heavenly family, who reunite just once a year.

23

AN INNOVATIVE AND ENTREPRENEUR SOCIETY

I was well aware of the fact that the Vietnamese are basically very innovative. During their War of Liberation they had innovated numerous indigenous methods to fight against the so called super powers of that time. It was only their daring endeavour to build a three layered underground, Cu Chi tunnel, that was spread over a few kilometers in deep forests and interesting aspect was that the enemy camp had no idea of it till its completion. That tunnel provided multidimensional services to the guerillas viz. shelter, medical treatment and provisions for lightning strikes over the enemy without allowing any time to recover. This author had an opportunity to visit the said tunnel on numerous occasions.

Not only during the liberation war but even after the liberation and reunification they continued to apply their innovative mind towards development and national reconstruction that is visible to any one in every part of Vietnam. It is amazing to observe that without disturbing the basic character of the old capital city Hanoi, how they have modernized it to make it more attractive for not only the Vietnamese but also for millions of tourists from all over the globe.

In most of Hanoi, the front portions of the shops are used for display of the wares while the rear portion is used by the shopkeepers for their family dwelling. Most of the families consist of three generations. This, in fact, is an old tradition of Vietnamese society, which they are still persisting with.

During last 20 years a new part of Hanoi has emerged which may compete with any global metropolis in its modernity and splendid facilities and comfort. There are numerous high rise buildings that provide office space and space for domestic habitation, besides big multistoreyed malls, food parks and places for amusement and entertainment. Special attention in town planning has also been given towards maintaining a healthy environment by providing small and big parks, fountains, open spaces, wide roads, and greenery. Thousands of trees are planted all over to make it a green city to provide fresh air to the inhabitants.

The Vietnamese are experimental by nature. They believe in the philosophy that says - do not carry the past and maintain whatever is there in accordance with the present situation and beneficial for the society.

They believe that conditions do change and so the nation and the society should not abstain from any change that is advantageous and useful for it. Thoughts, ideas and ethics may belong to anywhere else but what is the harm in adapting to it if those are worthwhile for the society. And so they easily adopted whatever they considered good of the western society leaving aside whatever was not suitable to their own society.

I may like to cite an example here in this context. The basic script of the Vietnamese language had been quite a difficult one and identical to the Mandarin, the script of the Chinese language. The Roman-based script that is presently used in Vietnam dates back to the 17th century. French, Portuguese and Spanish Catholic missionaries, aided by the Vietnamese preachers had developed a new easier writing system as a means of spreading it to a wider audience. The man credited with developing the current Roman based Chu Quoc Ngu (script of the national language) was Alexandre De Rhodes, a French Jesuit missionary, who had come to Vietnam in 1627. Within six months of his arrival, De Rhodes was reportedly preaching in fluent Vietnamese.

At first, Confucian scholars resisted the adoption of the new script. The spread of this easy to learn script undermined their power, which was based on traditional scholarship written in Han characters or chu nom. Later, budding nationalists also had reservations about quoc ngu calling it a worm-or-cricket-like script created by imperialists. But while few common people could read or write Chu Nom, the masses readily adopted Quoc Ngu. Thus, those same intellectuals who had first denounced the new script later saw it a convenient weapon in the fight against colonialism.

In the first half of the 20th century, the new script greatly facilitated contact between Vietnamese and Western cultures. Following Vietnam's independence from the French, Vietnamese Government officially recognized it as the nation's official writing system. Uncle Ho also advocated movement to Vietnamese words, and founded the Binh Dan Hoc Vu (Department for Popularizing Culture) to launch a campaign to eliminate illiteracy.

The usage of the newer script brought refinement also in the Vietnamese language and literature.

As mentioned earlier Ho Chi Minh was a great follower of Marxism and Leninism but while implementing the theory in practice in Vietnam he Vietnamized it and needless to say that it helped a lot in successfully establishing socialist system in Vietnam to a great extent.

So far as the entrepreneurship of the Vietnamese is concerned, they are matching with any fast developing country in Asia or developed country of Europe. It is worth mentioning that in the entrepreneurship skill the Vietnamese women are almost equal to the men.

In the production and export of tea, coffee, cashew nuts, black pepper, cinnamon Vietnam has surpassed many countries. In export of cashew nuts, black peper and cinnamon Vietnam ranks first in the world while it is the second largest exporter in Coffee and third largest exporter in rice.

In the chain of supermarkets and marts Vietnam is competeing with the world renowned supermarkets and most chains in their homeland and the same is the position in Café chains. Many renowned companies are unable to compete and are withdrawing.

In the year 2015 while I was on a visit to Vietnam along with my colleague Kusum Jain, we were staying at a Guest House of the Diplomatic Academy of Vietnam, Hanoi as the guest of Pravamayee Samantaray, who was teaching English there. One evening she informed us most enthusiastically that a new shopping mall VIN MART had come up in the vicinity at a ten minutes' walking distance from our Guest House. Next day we decided to visit the mall and spent there about two hours. It was an eye opening experience for us as we found quality products ranging from daily life items at most competitive and reasonable prices. The Vin Mart brand appeared officially in the market in November 2014.

Again in the year 2017 while passing through the road, I came across another Vin Mart Supermarket outlet. Naturally, I was reminded of my visit to one such Vin Mart outlet in 2015 and so I decided to step in. I was amazed to learn that within a short span of three years the VIN Group had opened more than 50 Supermarkets and around 900 Vin Marts nationwide with a mission 'For a better life for the Vietnamese'.

According to the experts the VIN Group will redraw and change the scenario of domestic retail market and create a balance for Vietnamese enterprises while facing a storm of occupying the market by foreign retail groups.

24

GLIMPSES OF LIFE IN VIETNAM

I am neither an academician nor a research scholar. I don't know how to play with the figures. I adopt simple ways to narrate the facts.

I write whatever I see with my open eyes and leave it to the readers to arrive at their own conclusion. A society's affluence may not be judged by individuals, but by the minimum living standard of the common man at the bottom line.

Traditional woman vendor Selling eatables.

A fruit vendor selling fruits on motorbike.

During the landing of my flight in Hanoi, Ho Chi Minh City or Da Nang, I saw water tanks made up of stainless steel shining on the roof tops without any exception. Even during my last visit to a remote mountainous village, I saw the same quality water tanks at the roof of the houses. I was told by a villager that sometimes they use it to store food grains and other fertilizers.

As already mentioned earlier, I had the opportunity to visit Vietnam for about 28 times between 1982 and 2017 in long span of 36 years. I had the honour of meeting and interacting with H. E. the General Secretary of the Communist Party of Vietnam, the Hon'ble President, the Prime Minister, the Chairperson of the National Assembly of Vietnam besides the legendary personalities viz. Hon'ble Pham Van Dong, General Vo Nguyen Giap and Madam Nguyen Thi Binh.

My numerous meetings and interactions were not only limited to high dignitaries and officials of Vietnam but I also had various occasions of having meetings and interactions with the common people of Vietnam besides having few occasions of meeting and staying with some Vietnamese families. I also had few heart to heart discussions with the intellectuals and literators of Vietnam that helped me a good deal to understand the political, social and cultural aspects of Vietnam.

I am writing all this to denote that I did not only have the occasions to understand in depth and from close quarters the political and economic system of Vietnam besides its geographical conditions, its culture, literature, family structure but also the psyche of the Vietnamese people which could not have been possible by going through only books and papers.

I had witnessed the phase between 1982 and 1985 when the Government and the people of Vietnam were endeavouring to overcome the unparalleled devastation in the history of mankind so that planned initiatives could be undertaken to ensure all round progress and development of the nation.

We had the occasion to visit and witness the agricultural fields that were turned barren due to Napalm and chemical bombings. It was nothing short of a nightmare to witness several villages, the total population of which had become physically challenged due to sprinkling of Orange chemical and it was feared that even the progeny would be affected by this destructive chemical. One can

An old woman selling her wares on the street.

Sweeping staff of municipolity collecting garbage.

witness its devastative effect even today at certain places. Even today there are government sponsored NGOs, who are looking after the survivors of the 'Orange Chemicals'. I was told that still there were quite a number of landmines lying undefused and that numerous people had already lost their lives in its explosions.

It is unparalleled in the history of mankind that from ruins a country has not only recovered but has become a front runner among the developing countries of the world. The devastation in Vietnam cannot be compared to that of Germany and Japan during the Second World War as both Germany and Japan were already developed nations and had a technological knowledge of their own. Further, the U.S. and its allied countries had extended sufficient material help towards their reconstruction. Vietnam on the other hand had been a French colony for about hundred years and economically it was one of the backward countries of the world.

Another fact that deserves mention here is that the U.S. was reluctant to accept its defeat at the hands of the Vietnamese and so its attitude and activities were being guided and run by a sense of vengeance and retribution. Till 1996 the U.S. and its allied countries had forced an economic blockade over Vietnam and had not granted it a diplomatic recognition. The biggest help provider to Vietnam was the Soviet Union that had disintegrated in 1990. Despite such diverse conditions Vietnam achieved remarkable all round development and the credit for which goes to the firm resolve of the ruling party - the Communist Party of Vietnam and the firm intention and committed endeavours of its people.

There are several areas where Vietnam is on top in Asia. Take Vietnamese women for instance. Vietnamese women are the most liberated ones in the Asian region. The Vietnamese society is almost free from feudalism. Yes, disparity is there in Vietnam but it's not an inhuman one. The distribution of wealth is more or less based on equality and justice.

So, unless one ponders over the aforesaid facts one may not be able to understand Vietnam and its society properly.

There is one more thing that deserves mention. The people of Vietnam are basically peace loving by nature but if any country challenges its sovereignty or captures its territory they are ever ready to retaliate with all their might unitedly.

We had the occasion to visit a rehabilitation centre in 1982 where vocational training was being provided to about 500 erstwhile

Grand parents enjoying their evening with their grandchild.

Dining Hall of a factory Where workers are having Lunch.

prostitutes to enable them to be economically self reliant to start life afresh and to join the mainstream society. It needs no mention here that before unification Ho Chi Minh City was known as Saigon and that it was considered to be the biggest brothel of Asia where there were about 500,000 prostitutes in 1975. Today, however, its place has been taken over by Bangkok.

During those times a greater section of the Vietnamese Society was reeling under intense conditions of poverty. For instance, due to pressing scarcity of newsprint and white print paper several students had to share the same book. Similarly, one newspaper was also shared by 15-20 readers and even classic literary work was published on newsprint, a paper inferior in quality.

Had I not been an eye-witness to all these, it would have been extremely difficult for me to comprehend and believe. Such an economically distressed society had not only recovered but has become a prosperous society in 2017. It is a fact and not at all an exaggeration.

How this miracle could be accomplished and that too in mere 30 years? Under the most practical Doi-Moi Policy, the national reconstruction work had started through Five Year Plans in the year 1990 and by 2017 the transformation of Vietnam into a fast developing nation was evident in almost all the areas, even in the distant hilly areas, of Vietnam. The fruits of the national progress and development reached to every citizen.

As mentioned earlier, in 1982 the mode of transport in Vietnam was cycle, a few bikes and very few cars. Now in 2017 cycle is almost obsolete, a few remained as a heritage for the foreign tourists. Each and every adult has a motor bike be it in city or in remote village. In Vietnam fifty five million motor bikes are on the roads (total population is ninety five million) and the numbers of cars in the city are hundreds of thousands and it is increasing day by day. Total public transport in Vietnam is air conditioned. The credit for such a great accomplishment, according to me, should go to the just, appropriate and inspiring leadership of Ho Chi Minh, the effect of which still persists despite certain drifts. The thoughts of Ho Chi Minh had a great impact on shaping the psyche of the people of Vietnam.

During all my visits to Vietnam, I gathered through my interactions with the local people that they least discuss about religion or interrelations among various ethnic groups. No myths are created about the past nor it is glorified. People realised it and appreciated as it was. They don't live in the past. People do have a sense of glory but they never boast.

People in Vietnam do not discuss much about the past or religion. On the contrary their principal concern is about the standard of living, corruption and social inequality. They bemoan, why despite hard labour their standard of living was lower as compared to that of the South Koreans. They believe, had there been no corruption, may be their life style would have been little better.

In Buddhism, despite the faith of the common man, people are not bigoted or fundamentalists towards religion. In fact, the younger generation of Vietnam declares itself to be humanists rather than believing in any faith. One may find nominal fatalism and some superstition here and there but most of the people have more faith on themselves and on the system and administration.

During a meeting with H.E. the President of Vietnam, I dared to ask 'How can you have a friendly relation with the U.S. that had led Vietnam to ruins and devastation?' His Excellency had replied - "It is true Mr. Sharma that the U.S. administration was instrumental in our devastation but a sizable section of the American society had still lent its moral support to us. We do not forget the past. We live in present, dream and visualize our future. If America invests in Vietnam and establishes industry on our terms and conditions, we know it well that they have come here not for charity but for profit, so what is the harm if it is helpful for our development and provides employment to our people. That is why we welcome the U.S.".
In 2017 while passing through Samsung factory situated in Thai Nguyen province, we learnt that Samsung had earned a huge profit, but it had also provided employment to about 250,000 Vietnamese people. It purchased water from the government of Vietnam besides paying a part of its income to the government as tax.

We also learnt about another episode where the Farmosa Company of Taiwan had polluted the Sea Water in an area to such an extent that the people of the area contacted various diseases, some even terminal, it affected the agriculture and led to death of millions of fishes and sea creatures. Finally, the government took initiative and penalized the company. Meanwhile, in the process, a scam was unearthed and a high official responsible for it was suspended from the service.

Vietnam today is one of the most prosperous nations in Asia, a status that it has achieved through sheer commitment, dedication and hard work of its people following the ideals and guidelines of the great leader President Ho Chi Minh. The progress of Vietnam reflects in the life style of its people. Most of the people in Vietnam prefer air travels; as a result almost all the airports in Vietnam are overcrowded. Road travels through luxury buses, cars and bikes

A manufacturing unit of 'North Star' bags owned by Madam Fiet.

are considered to be the second option while the third option before the people is railway travels. To attract more passengers and to promote railway travels the railways in Vietnam offer special rebates to those passengers, who book their travel tickets in advance.

It is very difficult to assess through outer appearance and attire, who is rich and who is poor in Vietnam, although in the recent years the disparity between the rich and the poor has increased and due to corruption the process of development seems to be choking at certain stages at the cost of the people and nature. Naturally, it causes imbalance and discontent among the society. Even the newspapers and media that are controlled to certain extent by the administration are of late vocal and are openly reporting this aspect. However, the steps that are being undertaken to eradicate corruption seem to be insufficient as compared to the extent/ volume of corruption. The increase in the number of luxury cars viz. B.M.W. and Mercedes etc. clearly point towards the increase in disparity among the people. The increase in number of Fashion Shows, Lifestyle Shows and exhibitions of luxury items that have become common in the Five Star Hotels and the tendency of patronizing club culture also indicate that an elitist society is

Enjoying dinner with a Vietnamese Family.

slowly and steadily gaining strength in Vietnam.

There had been a time in Vietnam when foreign tours were beyond the reach of common people. Conditions have changed now and quite a number of people visit foreign destinations for rest and recuperation. Substantial increase in the number of holiday resorts and hotels and their ever increasing occupancy is also a pointer towards the fact that presently even a commoner can afford this life style and on special family occasions they spend their time out at these resorts along with their families and friends. One of my Vietnamese friends had celebrated the ninetieth birth anniversary of his grandfather along with his family members and friends at one of such comfortable resorts.

People in Vietnam, I observed, enjoy their evenings out over dinner at numerous hotels and restaurants, that may look deserted during the day time but are overcrowded in the evenings. This is true with every restaurant and hotel, costly or not so costly. Every coffee-chain, be it 'Highlands' or 'Star Bucks' or an ordinary coffee shop or ice-cream parlour, are all usually overcrowded in the evening. We witnessed this phenomenon in Vietnam when we visited these places to enjoy a sip of coffee or an ice-cream or to have dinner with our Vietnamese as well as Indian friends. We found that our Vietnamese friends loved their drinks followed by buffet dinner. Needless to say, it is an indicator towards the affluent urban life style of the Vietnamese people.

Another thing that I observed was that when the orders were served in the hotels and restaurants of Vietnam, the amount of food served was so much in quantity that some wastage was inevitable. When we asked, our Vietnamese friends informed that the residual food will not be destroyed but would be collected in containers and would be sent to such agencies, who will feed it to the animals. We were told that every hotel had that arrangement.

We also wondered, how despite having sufficient food, our Vietnamese friends maintained their slim figures unlike the Americans and even Indians. We were, in fact, amazed to find our Vietnamese friends slim-trim, fit and without extra fat. Even the girls maintained their charm with 'zero figures'. We wondered, what was the secret? Our Vietnamese friends confided that there were three reasons for it. Firstly, the Vietnamese consume healthy food without much oil and spices. Mostly they eat lots of green vegetables, fish, chicken, meat with vegetable soups, rice and soya sauce, followed by fresh seasonal fruits and avoid sweets or desserts. Second reason for body fitness among the Vietnamese is their habit of hard work. Even in the household everybody works, not only the women. And the third reason of their fitness is their regular physical exercise, workouts and walking habit. In most of the cities in the mornings and evenings one may find a number of people engaged in physical exercises or walking in the parks; some parks have installed gym like equipments for exercises for common use.

Office time in Vietnam begins at 7:30 A.M. and ends at 5 P.M. with a lunch and resting recess of two hours from 11:30 A.M. to 1:30 P.M. when people have their lunch for an hour and then rest for an hour. Those who have their offices within 10 km. distance from their homes, easily go to their homes for lunch and rest during the recess and those who come from distant places take a nap after lunch in the office itself, that have necessary arrangements.

People in general in Vietnam rise early in the morning and have an early dinner at about 6 P.M. Yes, after early dinner they may go for a walk or a chit-chat session at a nearby coffee shop. This is the daily routine that is more or less followed by the people of Vietnam everywhere, in the cities, its suburbs and even in the country side. These days, however, due to family soaps over TV Channels, some people are confined to their households in the evening. Even children are becoming addict to cartoon channels and are developing a fancy towards pizzas, cake and junk food and as a result obesity, though slowly, is developing among them.

Provinces in Vietnam enjoy more autonomy. For example, every province has an import and export department of its own besides Department of Foreign Affairs. Authorities deal directly with any country regarding export, import and foreign relations. Powers are, however, limited and the key decisions rest with the centre.

Although Vietnam is a socialist country, yet they have adapted flexibility to adjust with the market economy prevailing all over the world. Around forty per cent of business and industry in Vietnam are in private sector but the key industries like defence production and the mineral and land on lease basis to private sector for housing, building factories etc. are in public sector.

Shopkeeper mother watching her children play on the pavement in front of her shop.

I witnessed that the government of Vietnam had allowed almost all the Multi National Corporations to establish their business and manufacturing units with the simple consideration that it was helpful for the economic growth of Vietnam.

Vietnam may not be a paradise on this earth. It does have its shortcomings, problems but the system has ensured a dignified life with basic amenities that many countries, especially in South Asia, may only dream about.

Since last twenty years, particularly after establishment of relations with the U.S. there has been massive penetration of American culture in Vietnamese society posing thereby a grave concern and challenge before the Vietnamese administration and thinkers, who all are engaged in thinking and devising ways and means to stop this infiltration. They have no allergy against the U. S. culture. Their principal concern is the perversion in the U.S. culture.

We are passing through a very complex world today where dedication, motivation, ideology that is beneficial to the mankind is getting irrelevant. Narrow nationalism is causing conflicts between the nations and a threat to the weaker nations is prevailing.

Alongside, terrorism inspired by religions is also becoming one of the biggest threats to the mankind and it has no barrier.

It, however, does not at all mean that there is no poverty. In fact about 10 per cent of the population in Vietnam is on or below the poverty line but everyone has a shelter or rather roof over one's head.

Yes, there is the welfare system in Vietnam but it does not suffice. We found people of age group between 70 and 75 years, doing some odd jobs to earn a living.

In Ho Chi Minh province about 6 per cent and in Da Nang about 3 per cent people are below the poverty line. The Government of Vietnam claims that by 2020 nobody will be there below the poverty line. Due to the fast pace of development in Vietnam during the last fifteen years the number of people below the poverty line has substantially decreased and so one wishfully hopes that by 2020 there would be none below the poverty line in Vietnam.

The craze for Massage Parlours and Sauna Bath centres in almost all the small and big cities of Vietnam is on the increase since last few years. During the weekends people also enjoy their nights out at Karaoke Bars, where they eat, drink, sing and dance almost all through the night without creating any nuisance whatsoever.

On the nights of Fridays and Saturdays, the people of various age groups, especially the youth, enjoy songs, dances and drinks till late nights and then return to their respective homes. Even girls are safe at nights and do not apprehend molestation.

So far as women empowerment is concerned, by and large, they are much ahead than their counterparts in any other Asian country which includes even Japan and South Korea.

Vietnamese women live their lives in their own way. They choose their partners and before tying the knot they do take blessings of their parents.

In transformation of Vietnamese society, economy and all-round development, women have almost equally contributed. They are totally free from the shackles of religion with exception among the Muslim communities.

Vietnam is a peaceful country engaged in its own development and needs peace for the same. Despite some of its shortcomings here and there it is steadily marching ahead and hopefully its stride continues in the years to come.

25

SNIPPETS

1. Apsara

As mentioned earlier, after visiting the Temple Tower sites in My Son visitors are taken to a small auditorium where 'Apsara Dance' is performed by a dancer for them. This dance form is derived from the sculptures of 'Apsara Dancers' sculpted in various dance postures on the walls and pillars of various Cham (Hindu) temple towers.

Logo of Apsara Restaurant Da Nang.

Apsara is a name that charms the Vietnamese and foreign visitors. There is also a restaurant named 'Apsara' in Da Nang, which I visited several times during my various journeys. The walls of the said restaurant are decorated with various sculptures of Apsaras in dancing postures and during the dinner time the guests are entertained by a beautiful dancer dressed as an 'Apsara' by her sensual Apsara dance.

A Terracotta idol of Apsara.

Apsara is so popular in Vietnam that in ancient towns like Hoi An, Hue, My Son, Da Nang etc. the terracotta models of Apsara are sold in souvenir shops in a very big number.

According to the Indian mythology 'Apsaras' are the dancing girls in the court of Indra, the king of gods in the Vedic period. They were used by Indra and other gods of Pauranic period to break the meditation of saints, who wished to go to heaven in their life time. Sometimes Apsaras were cursed for certain deeds of their own and were sent to the earth from heaven for a certain period.

In southern India almost in every Hindu temple there are sculptures of Apsaras in their various dance postures, which are copied in the Hindu (Cham) Temples in Vietnam.

APSARA
THE DANCER OF CHAMPA

She oversleeps in the kalpa of stone
Born from the artist's hands
A hundred years turn into a moment of time
A dream is smouldering relentlessly for thousands of years.

She stirs herself from the womb of stone
With an ineffable smile on her lips
In the image of a dancer
She wanders through the journey on earth.

Tomorrow she returns to the realm of stone
With her exquisite curves of wonder
A skand turns into eternity
She gives humankind nostalgia between earth and sky.

By PHU TRAM (INRASARA), Cham poet and scholar
(Source: S. E. A. Write Anthology of Asean Short Stories & Poems The 30th Anniversary)

2. New site discovered at Da Nang

During the construction of a building at a site at Phong Le, about

New Cham site discovered at Phong Le Near Da Nang.

New Cham site discovered at Phong Le Near Da Nang.

10 kms. from Da Nang City while a plot of land was being dug for laying the foundation some huge slabs of stones that appeared to be a part of some ancient structure were unearthed. Within minutes the news spread all over the city like a fire in the wilderness. As and when the news reached Mr. Vo Van Thang, the Director of Da Nang Museum For Cham Sculptures, he rushed to the said site along with a team of archaeologists who inspected the style of structures, sculptures and architectural decorative elements found at the site to hypothesize the date of the discovered structure to be between 10th and 12th centuries. They believed it to be the 'gate temple' (gopuram) of a group of Cham temples.

On request and advice of the team of archaeologists, the Government of Vietnam took over the possession of the site, covered it by corrugated sheets and appointed a care-taker to look after the artifacts that were found at the site.

The Director of Da Nang Museum For Cham Sculptures Mr. Thang seemed to be very excited about the discovery and the excavated artifacts and he submitted a project to the Government to develop

New Cham site discovered at Phong Le Near Da Nang.

the site as heritage and tourist attraction. The Government has agreed in principle to implement his project according to which a museum, a café, and souvenir shops will be built at the site besides a beautiful lake with clusters of lotus flowers, that would be linked and connected with River Han, to make it a big attraction for the tourists, who may visit the site even by boat from Da Nang. It may take about five years for completion of the project. The adjoining houses and areas of the site have been requisitioned for beautification of the area.

This project will enjoin the golden past of the city with the modern one.

3. Raising Trionychild Turtles

The commune of Khai Thai in Phu Xuyen District Hanoi, had been once a very poor area with sandy soil due to which cultivation of crops was quite difficult, yet the locals had to mainly live by rice farming and it was difficult for them to evade conditions of poverty.

There is a popular saying 'If there is a will, there is a way'. War veteran Tran Bang and his family were strong willed people, who were resolute in their will to overcome poverty. When they got an information and idea about raising turtles, Bang saw high economic return from the species as its demand was increasing in the market. He believed that his profit may even double after two years of toil despite a large amount of initial capital required to pay for the labour, breeding and feeding of the turtles.

With great determination he borrowed money to hire labourers for dredging his 200 sq. mtrs. Pond and to buy turtles for breeding and their food. After ten years his determination has paid dividends and today he is a name to reckon with for raising turtles and he has helped many of his fellow locals to develop the business.

(Source: Raising Trionychild Turtles in Khai Thai' by Thuc Hien published in Vietnam Pictorial No. 694-10/2016)

26

OVERVIEW

The Democratic Republic of Vietnam was founded after the 1945 August Revolution, when President Ho Chi Minh declared independence. The Socialist Republic of Vietnam has been the official name since 1976.

Vietnam is located on the eastern seaboard of the Indochina peninsula, sharing common borders with China to the north, and Laos and Cambodia to the west. To the east and south lies the East Sea. Mountains and hills cover Four-fifths of Vietnam's territory with the Truong Son Range stretching over 1,400km. Mount Fansipan (3.142m) is the highest peak on mainland Southeast Asia. The most populated areas in Vietnam are the Red River Delta and the Mekong Delta, which feature fertile soil fed by a dense river network. Vietnam's territorial waters cover over 1,000,000 km. The country's coastline stretches' for 3,444 km. and offers many stunning tropical beaches. Vietnam's total area is 331.690 sq. km.

RESOURCES

Minerals: coal, iron, aluminum, tin, and oil. Agricultural and Forestry products: rice, maize, sweet potatoes, peanuts, soya beans, rubber, lacquer, coffee, tea, tobacco, cotton, coconut, sugarcane, jute, and tropical Fruit. Vietnam also produces and exports readymade garments, leather shoes, ladies sandals, handbags etc.

CLIMATE

Vietnam's climate varies a great deal from north to south. Northern

Vietnam has Four distinct seasons: spring, summer, autumn and winter. In the north, summers are warm, while winters are cool and misty. Southern Vietnam is warm all year-round, with temperatures typically varying by just three degrees Celsius. Tropical monsoons occur From May to October in the north and south, and From September to January in the Central Region.

ADMINISTRATIVE DIVISIONS

Vietnam has 63 provinces, including five municipalities (Hanoi, Ho Chi Minh City, Haiphong, Can Tho, Da Nang).

ETHNIC GROUPS

There are 54 ethnic groups living in Vietnam. The Viet (or Kinh) people account for 88% of Vietnam's population and are mostly concentrated in the lowlands. Most of the country's 5.5 million ethnic minority people live in mountainous areas. Major groups include the Tay; the Nung; the Thai; the Muong; the H'mong; the Dao; the Hoa; the Khmer; the Bana; the Giarai; and the Ede.

RELIGIONS

Major spiritual influences in Vietnam include Buddhism, Taoism, Confucianism, and native religions (Ancestor, Mother Goddess Worship). Christianity arrived in the late 18th century and now has the second largest following, after Buddhism. Other religions practised include Islam and Cao Dai, with higher concentrations in the South.

VIETNAMESE LANGUAGE AND SCRIPTS

More than 80% of the population speak Vietnamese (or Kinh), the national language. Ethnic minorities have native languages. Three scripts have influenced Vietnam's history: Han (classical Chinese) ideograms were used until the beginning of the 20th century. The Nom script, created between the 11th and 14th centuries, is based on the Han script. European missionaries in the 17th century used the Roman alphabet to record the Vietnamese language and created Quoc Ngu script. After independence in 1945, Quoc Ngu was developed and used as the official national language.

MEETINGS

[meetings and interactions with higher dignitaries to common people in vietnam between 1982 to 2017]

VISIT TO VIETNAM ON GOODWILL MISSION 1982

In the Picture (Left to Right)
Activists of Vietnam Communist Party.
Ajit Pande, President of Vietnam Friendship League, Prof. Suranjan Das, Nirmal Chowdhury,
Phom Phan Dang (Prime Minister of Vietnam), Ajay De, Prof. Santimoy Roy, Interpretor, Geetesh Sharma,
Secretary, Vietnam Friendship League.

With H.E. Mr. Nong Duc Manh, then Seeretary General of the Communist Party of Vietnam and other delegates at an International Seminar on Ho Chi Minh at Hanoi on 13th May 2010.

H.E. Mr. Truong Tan Sang, then president of S.R. Vietnam discussing some point with the author while (from L to R) Ms. Kusum Jain, H.E. Mr. Ranjit Rai, then Ambassador of india in Vietnam, Mr. Prem Kapoor and Mr. Vu Xuan Hong, then President of VUFO.

With H.E. Mr. Huynh Dam, then Chairman, People's Committee of Ho Chi Minh City.

With H.E, Truong Minh Tuan, Minister for information & Communication and Chairman of VIFA.

With Ms. Nguyen Thi Binh, 2005, Hanoi.

Mr. Le Chi Thanh, then Vice Chairman, HUFO, Presenting the Author 'Medal of Friendship' at HCM City on 1st December 2004.

With H.E. Mr. Tran Van Minh, Vice Chairman People's Committee of Da Nang City in 2017 at the newly built Administrative Building.

The Author addressing a meeting of INCHAM to Welcome the delegation of Howrah Chamber of Commerce the first business delegation from Kolkata to NC Mcity in 2001.

The Author along with Ms. Kusum jain with Delbagh Mohan Singh, President, INCHAM, and Mr. M.B. Radhakrishnan, Vice President, INCHAM, in June 2017

Author with his colleagues and Vietnamese Writers (from L to R) Nguyen Linh Khien, Mr. Hai Thanh, Ms. Pravamayee Samantaray, Ms. Thuy, Author, Ms. Di Li, Ms. Kusum Jain.

After an interaction with the students of Hanoi University.

VIETNAM IN KOLKATA

The Author along with Prof. Santimoy Roy, founder of IVSC, Ms. Kusum Jain and other members of the Committee with Vietnam's legendary military strategist Gen. Vo Nguyen Giap and Madam Giap on the occasion of Birth Ceatenary of President Ho chi Minh at kolkata in 1990.

The Author felicitating and presenting a citation to H.E. Mr. Nguyen Xuan Phuc, then Dy. Prime Minister (Presently the Prime Minister) of S.R. Vietnam in New Delhi in 2013.

Dr. Karan Singh Signing the first copy just after the release of the book 'Traces of Indian Culture in Vietnam' and the Author in 2009.

Mr. Bikash Ranjan BhattaCharya, then Mayor, Kolkata Municipal Corporation inaugurating an exhibition of "Glimpses of Brahmanical Temples and Sculptures in Vietnam" by the Author (extreme right), organized by Indian Museum, Kolkata on 24th June 2009 at Asutosh birth centenary hall (Indian Museum), While Dr. K.K. Basa, then Director, Indian Museum (on left of Mr. Bhattacharya) look on.

Mr. Pavan Poddar, then President of Bharat Chamber of Commerce felicitating H.E. Mr. Vu Quang Diem, then Ambassador of Vietnam in India at a Luncheon Session in Kolkata in 2010.

The Author with Mr. Tridib Chattopadhyaya, Secretary General, Book Sellers and Publishers Guild and H.E. Mr. Nauyen Thanh Tan, then Ambassador of Vietnam in India at the 'Kolkata International Book Fair after inauguration of Vietnam Pavition in 2012.

H.E. Mr. Keshari Nath Tripathi, Governor of West Bengal unveiling Ho Chi Minh Plaque along with H.E. Mr. Ton sinh Thanh, Ambassador of Vietnam in India at the Lalit Great Eastern Hotel, Kokkata (where Ho Chi Minh stayed for one night on his way to paris in 1946) held on 26th August 2015.

The Author receiving 'order of Friendship' the highest civil Award to a foreigner by the Government of Vietnam, H.E. Mr. Ton Sinh Thanh, Ambassador of Vietnam in India in the presence of former Speaker of west Bengal Assembly Late Mr. Hashim Abdul Halim, who presided over the fanction at Hotel Hindusthan International in Kolkata on 19th May 2015.

Eminent Film Director Mr. Goutam Ghosh, Dr. Arun Kumar Chakraborti, Director General of National Library, Writer Karuna Pande, Mr. Amalesh Das Gupta, the Author and Ms. Kusum Jain inside the Vietnam Pavilion at Kolkata International Book Fiar 2017.

A Seminar on 'Relevance of Ho Chi Minh in Present Complex World' on Ho Chi Minh's 12th Birth Anniversary held at the Lalit Great Eastern Hotel on 19th May 2017. Speakers on Dais from L to R are Mr. Goutam De, Regional Director, ICCR, Kolkata, Ms. Phuong Vu. Counseller, cultural and Political, Embassy of Vietnam in India, Ms. Deepika Pokharna, Director (Library), Ministry of culture, Govt. of India, the Author, Dr. Arun Kumar Chakraborty, Director, National Library, H.E. Mr. Eaknarayan Aryal, Consul Genral of Nepal in Kolkata.